Self-Esteem for Men

An Essential Self-Help Guide to Building Alpha Male Habits that will Improve Your Mental Toughness, Confidence, and Ability to Attract Women

© Copyright 2020 - All rights reserved.

The contents of this book may not be reproduced, duplicated, or transmitted without direct written permission from the author.

Under no circumstances will any legal responsibility or blame be held against the publisher for any reparation, damages, or monetary loss due to the information herein, either directly or indirectly.

Legal Notice:

You cannot amend, distribute, sell, use, quote, or paraphrase any part of the content within this book without the consent of the author.

Disclaimer Notice:

Please note the information contained within this document is for educational and entertainment purposes only. No warranties of any kind are expressed or implied. Readers acknowledge that the author is not engaging in the rendering of legal, financial, medical, or professional advice. Please consult a licensed professional before attempting any techniques outlined in this book.

By reading this document, the reader agrees that under no circumstances is the author responsible for any losses, direct or indirect, which are incurred as a result of the use of the information contained within this document, including but not limited to errors, omissions, or inaccuracies.

Contents

INTRODUCTION 1
PART ONE: SELF-ESTEEM 2
CHAPTER 1: SELF-ESTEEM EXPLAINED 3
CHAPTER 2: COMMON FEARS AND INSECURITIES MEN HAVE 10
CHAPTER 3: SELF-DOUBT; IDENTIFYING AND THWARTING YOUR WORST ENEMY 15
CHAPTER 4: BODY-IMAGE ANXIETY, AND FOUR WAYS TO OVERCOME IT 20
CHAPTER 5: FIVE WAYS TO BOOST YOUR SELF-ESTEEM NOW 25
PART TWO: ALPHA MALE HABITS 30
CHAPTER 6: THE ALPHA MALE PROFILE 31
CHAPTER 7: WHY WOMEN PREFER ALPHAS 36
CHAPTER 8: ALPHA MALE HABIT #1: CONFIDENCE 42
CHAPTER 9: ALPHA MALE HABIT #2: PERSISTENCE 48
CHAPTER 10: ALPHA MALE HABIT # 3: FRAME 52
CHAPTER 11: ALPHA MALE HABIT # 4: PHYSICAL APPEARANCE 56
CHAPTER 12: ALPHA MALE HABIT # 5: MENTAL TOUGHNESS 61
CHAPTER 13: ALPHA MALE HABIT # 6: CHARM 66
CHAPTER 14: ALPHA MALE HABIT # 7: PURPOSE 70
CHAPTER 15: ALPHA MALE HABIT # 8: SELF-CARE 75
CHAPTER 16: SETTING ALPHA MALE GOALS 80
CONCLUSION 85
SOURCES 87

Introduction

Although known by different names, the image of the Alpha Male is one that has been around for countless generations. In more recent times, this image has been linked to success in all areas of life, resulting in an ever-growing number of books, classes, and videos on the subject. Unfortunately, many of these books and videos contain common misconceptions about the true nature of an Alpha Male. As such, they provide a false direction to those pursuing the Alpha lifestyle. They may provide only a handful of qualities and skills needed to become an Alpha Male, causing confusion and frustration. This book takes the time to dispel all the false images of a true Alpha Male, painting a clear and concise picture that will help you to better understand the goal you are trying to achieve. Furthermore, it will provide all the steps you need to take to begin eliminating the bad habits that have held you back your whole life, as well as the steps needed to develop the winning habits of an Alpha Male. By the time you finish reading this book, not only will you know what it truly means to be an Alpha Male, but you will have all the tools needed to transform yourself into one.

Part One: Self-Esteem

Chapter 1: Self-Esteem Explained

Self-esteem is the very foundation of a person's success. Without it, you can never hope to achieve anything worthwhile in life. Everything from finding the right job to forming happy and meaningful relationships relies on you having a strong, vibrant sense of self-esteem. Unfortunately, this is one area where most men struggle. In fact, most of the things that undermine their efforts at achieving high levels of self-esteem are those very things that pose as the ideals they are striving for. Images of men with ripped muscles, beautiful women, and bags of cash, although inspiring for a time, can eventually cause you to see yourself as less successful, less attractive, and ultimately less capable, leaving your self-esteem shattered. Seemingly ordinary habits can also lead to an erosion of your sense of self, causing you to lack the confidence and motivation needed to take your life to the levels you desire. Fortunately, once you recognize these false images and bad habits for what they are, you can eliminate the negative impact they have on your overall wellbeing. This chapter will explore some of the more common causes of low self-esteem, and the devastating effects they can have on your life. Additionally, it will provide a questionnaire enabling you to determine whether or not you suffer from low self-esteem. Finally, you will be shown four fundamental ways that are proven to develop the highest levels of self-esteem, levels reserved for the Alpha Male.

The True Nature of Self-Esteem

Before getting into the symptoms and causes of low self-esteem, a clear definition of self-esteem is needed. Most people confuse the terms "self-esteem" and "self-confidence", assuming that they are the same thing. While these two elements are closely linked, they are, in fact, two very distinct and different things. Self-confidence is the belief in your ability to be able to do a certain thing. If you have strong self-confidence, you will take more chances, believing that you can succeed. For example, you might approach a beautiful woman in a bar because you are highly confident in your ability to form a connection and start a relationship. , if you have low self-confidence, you will probably avoid such interaction as you believe your chances of failure far outweigh your chances of success.

Self-esteem, although related, is something different altogether. When you have high self-esteem, you have a high sense of self-worth. You believe that you are capable of achieving your goals, which is where self-confidence fits in. However, you also have a positive self-image, believing that your looks and overall style are things to be proud of, elements that will attract the right woman or help you in your effort to land the right job. Additionally, you will have a strong sense of self-worth in terms of your values, ethics, and other life fundamentals that give you a sense of pride in everything you do. Self-confidence is an integral part of self-esteem, but it is only a part and not the entirety.

The best way to understand the true nature of self-esteem as opposed to self-confidence is to reduce them to their simplest terms. Self-confidence can best be expressed by the statement, "I can." In contrast, self-esteem can best be expressed by the statement "I am." Self-confidence describes what you can do, while self-esteem describes who you are. Again, although self-confidence is a critical element of self-esteem, it is but one element. Many other elements go into creating the overall picture of self-esteem —the image you have of yourself and the value your life possesses.

Common Signs of Low Self-Esteem

Low self-esteem can come in many forms and can be caused by any number of factors. Fortunately, diagnosing the basic condition is relatively easy to do. Since low self-esteem is a generally negative condition, any and all negative habits or outlooks on life will usually point to it. Some of the more common signs that you might be struggling with low self-esteem include the following:

- **Image Shame:** This is when you are self-conscious about your overall appearance, either in terms of your body or in terms of your style. Sometimes this happens when you compare your current appearance with images of what is considered as the ideal male. These can be images of a muscular, tanned figure who looks more like a Greek statue than an actual human being, making the average male feel inferior when seeing their physique in the mirror. They can also come in the form of the well-groomed, flawless model wearing the latest fashions and attracting the most beautiful women imaginable. Such images will only serve to make the average person feel ashamed of their appearance compared to that of the airbrushed model in the image staring down at them.

- **Performance Anxiety:** This is when you feel stressed about not meeting other people's expectations. Sometimes this shows up in relationships where a man is worried about not satisfying his significant other. He may be afraid of not "wowing" his woman in bed, or not having enough money, style, or emotional experience to satisfy a woman's needs. Outside of relationships, performance anxiety affects millions of men in the workplace, the gym, and other areas in life where being the best seems somehow expected of everyone.

- **Isolation:** If you find that you avoid social encounters, preferring to remain alone, you might have low self-esteem. It is one thing to enjoy some quiet time in solitude, but it is quite another to avoid social gatherings because you don't feel good enough about yourself to be seen in public.

- **Self-Deprecation:** While the occasional self-deprecating joke can be a healthy way to ease tension with others, or to avoid appearing arrogant, making a habit of such jokes can point to a low sense of self-worth. This is especially true if those jokes cause discomfort rather than the laughs they are intended to generate.

- **A Lack of Desire for Self-Improvement:** This may seem a bit odd at first. After all, if you have high self-esteem, why would you want to improve yourself? However, the truth is that someone with a high sense of self-worth will always look for ways to become better, like a rich person always looking to make more money. The only reason you don't want to improve yourself is that you don't believe that you can.

- **Negative Expression:** Low self-esteem will show up in your language. Your body language will be negative, revealing uncertainty and anxiety. You will tend to say negative things, such as referring to goals as "impossible" or "unreasonable". You will never show enthusiasm when tackling something new or outside of your comfort zone.

While these are just a few of the more common signs of low self-esteem, they are easy to detect in your day-to-day life. The following questionnaire will help you to identify some of the more subtle ways that these causes may be presenting themselves in your life. If your answer is "yes" to most of the following questions, your self-esteem is low and needs to be fixed.

1. Do you avoid social interactions whenever possible, due to a sense of anxiety or shame?

2. Do you rely on using alcohol or some other substance to reduce anxiety and give you the courage to face your fears?

3. Do you often feel self-conscious about your physical appearance?

4. Is it hard for you to accept compliments from others?

5. Are you often overly apologetic, even for things that aren't your fault?

6. Do you avoid offering your opinion for fear that you will be ridiculed or found lacking intellectually?

7. Do you ignore personal grooming?

8. Are you surprised when people are happy to see you?

9. Do you constantly fish for compliments or validation?

10. Are you unable to make quick, specific decisions?

11. Are you suspicious of people who want to spend time with you?

12. Is your mind filled with doubt and memories of past failure?

13. Are you constantly comparing yourself to everyone around you?

14. Are you single or in a miserable relationship?

15. Are you unhappy with your job?

16. Are you unhappy in your life?

Common Causes of Low Self-Esteem

If you answered "yes" to most of the questions listed above, then you have low self-esteem. Hearing that may only make you feel worse at first, but the good news is that it probably isn't your fault at all. In fact, most people with low self-esteem have become that way as a result of their environment. For example, if you spend your time with negatively minded people, who constantly belittle one another as well as themselves, then you can't help but begin to feed into that negativity. After a while, your self-esteem will plummet, leaving you to take on the negative world view that those people share. Even if those people are your friends, the impact they have on your life can be devastating, making them, in fact, your worst enemies.

A person's upbringing can also impact their sense of self in a very real way. Parents who are abusive or neglectful will leave their children scarred for life, lacking the self-esteem that children of loving, positive parents have in abundance. This is because a person's self-image is largely learned. Therefore, if you grew up with your parents telling you that you are stupid, ugly, or a disappointment, then you will develop that belief. You will see yourself through their filters, focusing on your perceived faults, flaws, and shortcomings. In the end, these are the only things you will see, resulting in a complete lack of self-esteem.

Past experiences can also go a long way toward undermining your self-esteem. This goes hand-in-hand with self-confidence. If, for example, you try to lose ten pounds by going on a particular diet, but fail to achieve your goal, your self-confidence will take a hit. If you try two, three, or four other diets and continue to fall short of achieving your goals, you may be tempted to feel as though you simply aren't good enough to lose those ten pounds no matter what you do. Unfortunately, it only takes two or three failed attempts for most people before they give up, blaming themselves for their lack of success.

Finally, there is the issue of toxic stereotypes. Modern-day marketing has discovered that the best way to sell a product is to shame a person into buying it. This is why only the prettiest women model makeup or the latest fashions, while the most muscular or flawless men show off exercise equipment or the latest in men's fashions. In the end, it is the sense of feeling inferior to the models that make most people buy the clothes, the makeup, or the exercise machine. Unfortunately, none of those things ever transform the individual into the image in the picture, leaving them to give up, feeling inadequate, disappointed, and inferior.

Four Ways to Build Alpha Male Self-Esteem

If you have ever found yourself in any of these situations, take heart; you are not alone. Millions of men all around the world suffer from low self-esteem. Fortunately, none of the causes are without a cure. In fact, the path to recovery is often faster and easier than the path that led you to low self-esteem in the first place. The trick is to get to the heart of the problem rather than just trying to fix the symptoms. By curing the disease, you will eliminate the symptoms, leaving you with the high self-esteem that you need to achieve the success and happiness you both crave and deserve. The following are four ways to build Alpha Male self-esteem.

- **Develop Self-Awareness:** Ignoring problems usually doesn't do much toward solving them. The first step is to take the time to examine your feelings and to discover their causes. Address your fears, your doubts, and your regrets. Write them down so that you can begin to take control of them. Look them straight in the face and recognize the impact they have had on your life.

- **Address your Issues:** Once you have identified the issues that rob you of your self-esteem, the next step is to begin overcoming them. In the case of feeling ashamed of your appearance, recognize that you can change your appearance. Take the time to decide how you want to look, and then find every available resource that will help you achieve that goal. In the case of losing weight, find a gym, get a membership, and find a personal trainer or coach who can guide you so that you get the most from your effort. If it's a better job you want or better success at attracting women, figure out the areas you need to develop and begin pursuing those things. Find friends or life coaches who can offer insights and guidance, as well as an ear to bend when things don't go according to plan. In short, tackle your problems wholeheartedly.

- **Change your Story:** Once you have identified your issues and start to overcome them, you can begin to change your inner dialogue. Gone are the days of you not being good enough for success. Now that you are making strides in overcoming the things that robbed you of self-esteem, you can begin to feel better about yourself. Every victory, no matter how small, is a victory nonetheless, and it is worth celebrating. Even before you begin to lose weight, you can celebrate joining a gym, finding a coach, and developing a plan that will help you to achieve your goal. In short, you can celebrate taking charge of your life and changing course from failure to fulfilling your dreams.

- **Create the Big Picture:** Change comes in small, incremental measures at first. This is why it is vital to celebrate every win, no matter how small. However, you won't want to settle for small gains for long. Instead, you will want to create a bigger picture, the overall goal you hope to achieve with these small wins. For example, losing ten pounds might just be the beginning; you might want to start developing your muscles, getting some tone, and shaping a body that will give you pride when you go to the beach. Or you might want to change your style, buying clothes to show off your new shape, changing your hair cut for a more modern, fashionable look, or other similar changes. The important thing is to set your sights on the big prize, the ultimate goal. That will ensure that you stay motivated while remaining on the course that leads to your destination of life-changing success.

Chapter 2: Common Fears and Insecurities Men Have

To effectively fight any war, the first thing you need to do is to know your enemy. The fight for self-esteem is no exception to this rule. The only way you will be able to raise your levels of self-esteem to those of an Alpha Male is to identify the elements that serve to undermine your self-esteem in the first place. Only by removing and overcoming those obstacles will you be able to achieve your goal of self-transformation. Fortunately, the fears and insecurities that hinder your success are the same with which millions of other men all around the world struggle. So, they are well known, as are the methods for overcoming them. This chapter will deal with the fears and insecurities themselves, including how to identify them and what impact they have on your overall health and wellbeing. Only by knowing your own personal demons will you be able to choose the right methods of improvement from those offered in the rest of the book, thereby giving yourself the absolute best chance for success.

Inferior Physical Appearance

When it comes to self-esteem, few things are as vital as physical appearance. After all, your looks are more often than not the first thing anyone experiences about you. Even before they get to know your personality, your abilities, or your beliefs, they know what you look like. Although many would say not to judge a book by its cover, almost everyone does, and to a large degree. As a result, most men have serious fears and insecurities when it comes to their physical appearance.

The most commonly reported issue in this area comes in the form of the overall physique. Due to the increasingly sedentary nature of most lifestyles, it becomes harder and harder to keep unwanted weight off. Most men carry a few extra pounds around their waist, at the very least. While this isn't always a deal-breaker for most women, it is something that popular culture demonizes, especially within the advertising industries. Therefore, it is very common for men to feel self-conscious about their weight and their lack of muscle tone.

Another common fear concerning physical appearance is about one's hair. Baldness, although becoming more and more popular, is still seen as a non-Alpha Male trait. This is particularly true in the process leading up to baldness, namely the dreaded receding hairline. Men who experience thinning hair struggle with self-esteem, seeing it as a sign of their mortality and the fading of their masculinity. Other hair issues include chest or back hair. Some men feel that a lack of chest hair looks effeminate, while others are self-conscious about having too much body hair. There is no single measure by which the proper amount of body hair is defined, and this should not cause men to feel insecure.

A man's height can have a debilitating effect on his self-image. Tall men often feel exposed, as though they are the center of attention, whether or not they want to be. On the other end of the spectrum, short men often feel inferior, creating the well-known Napoleon Complex where short men have to prove themselves against their taller counterparts. Surprisingly enough, average-sized men can feel insecure due to their lack of distinction. Therefore, any and every height can affect a man in a very real and negative way, causing a problem that can't be readily resolved since you can't really change your height.

Inferior Performance

Even if you are lucky enough to feel perfectly happy with your physical appearance, including your height, your hair, and your weight, you still have to face the next obstacle, namely that of performance. The truth of the matter is that men are hardwired to be competitive. This can be traced back to primitive humans and the need to "win" a mate, either by brute force or by demonstrating better ability than other males present. Contests for females can be observed throughout nature, including birds singing and showing off bright plumage, primates challenging for dominance, or any number of species sparring to win the heart of the on-looking female. Although human culture and technology have advanced, human biology is still very much the way it was back in the days of our primitive cavemen ancestors. Therefore, the need to outperform every other male is alive and well in human males today.

Understandably, the main area where the need to outperform can be found is in the mating ritual itself. Countless men feel insecure when it comes to pleasing their woman in bed. This accounts for why porn is so popular. Numerous studies have shown that many men rely on porn for inspiration, hoping to learn tips and tricks to use to please their partners better. Most men still struggle with the fear that they aren't the best in that all-important arena. This is especially true in the case where their partner has had other lovers in the past. The fear of not matching up to former lovers can crush a man's spirit, and in a world where premarital sex is becoming the norm, such scenarios are becoming more and more common.

Another area where inferior performance is a very real fear is in providing for the family. Having a high paying, respectable job is the ideal for most men; when a man feels as though his job performance is inferior, he can struggle with self-esteem issues. Buying a bigger house, a flashier car, and having all the latest toys and gadgets can be either a way to overcome this fear or a way to show off when a man feels as though he is getting it done. However, such shows of vanity are more often than not an attempt to hide the deeper fears and insecurities of not always being the best when it comes to providing money and comfort for a man's family.

Performance fears can take many other forms, such as having to be the best at your job, a sport you play, or a hobby you enjoy. In the end, those things that are supposed to bring you joy and fulfillment can instead provide all sorts of opportunities to feel inferior and insecure. Needing to be the absolute best is a clear sign that you aren't secure in your natural ability but require the validation that being first can bring about. Likewise, needing to dominate at your job demonstrates a lack of security when it comes to your skills at work. In a society that is becoming faster paced and ever more competitive, the fear of not being good enough is becoming more and more widespread with each passing year.

Five Signs You Are Insecure

Sometimes fears and insecurities can be masked by behaviors that appear to be confident and strong. Such behaviors can leave the underlying causes of fear and insecurity unchecked, and the person's self-esteem continuing to be eaten away. Fortunately, the signs of insecurity are relatively easy to recognize. The following are five signs that you might be struggling with insecurity and low self-esteem:

- **Dishonesty:** No one likes a liar. When a person lies, they are covering up a truth they don't want to admit to or face. Therefore, if you find yourself lying to people regularly, it points to insecurity. This is particularly true if you lie about such things as your financial situation, your job, your skillset, or past experiences. If you have to invent stories to impress someone, you are insecure about your true self.

- **Being Needy:** The needier a person is, the less self-assured they are. After all, if you were a capable person with high self-esteem you wouldn't need other people to validate your life or take care of you. Neediness can come in many forms, including a sense of being helpless on your own, needing constant praise or validation from others, jealousy, rage, or other similarly unhealthy emotions that serve to undermine any relationship.

- **Extreme Introversion:** While being introverted in and of itself is not a sign of insecurity, extreme introversion is. The difference is in the nature of the introversion itself. If you prefer a quiet evening at home with your spouse or loved ones as opposed to going out on the town, that is not a bad thing. However, if you close yourself away from any and all human contact, that is a different situation altogether. Avoiding human contact is usually a sign of insecurity, and if you actively avoid social interaction, you need help rebuilding your sense of self-esteem.

- **Avoiding Eye Contact:** Social interaction is pretty much unavoidable, especially in the workplace, the grocery store, or any other place where you need to be regularly to sustain your day-to-day life. You can't hide insecurity when exposed to such social interactions. This is particularly true when it comes to eye contact. While a confident person will be able to maintain healthy and meaningful eye contact with someone they are talking to or listening to, someone struggling with insecurity will avoid such eye contact, much the way they would avoid social interaction altogether, given the choice.

- **Bullying Behavior**: The last sign of insecurity is one of the most misunderstood of them all, namely bullying behavior. It's natural to assume that a bully is someone confident of their capabilities; in fact, many aspects of bullying are wrongly attributed to the Alpha Male personality. The truth of the matter is that bullying behavior is a mask for serious insecurity. Most bullies are trying to keep others from noticing their low self-esteem; for that reason, they usually target people who personify their insecurities. Thus, if you pick on people who appear weak or who are different in one form or another, this is a sign that you are very insecure, and that your self-esteem needs a lot of work. Rather than being an Alpha Male, you are a poster child for fear and self-loathing, and have a complete lack of self-confidence.

The following checklist outlines the most common signs of insecurity. If you answer "yes" to most of the following, you need to keep reading, as your self-esteem needs to have a serious overhaul.

1. You wonder whether or not you are better than any lover from your significant other's past.

2. You lie about your finances, your job, or your past accomplishments.

3. You fixate on past successes, defining yourself by them.

4. You struggle to maintain eye contact with people.

5. You pick on or bully others, especially those you are secretly jealous of.

6. You rely on help from others for even the simplest of things.

7. You constantly compare yourself to others, feeling jealous and inferior as a result.

Chapter 3: Self-Doubt; Identifying and Thwarting Your Worst Enemy

When it comes to success, few things are as crucial as a strong sense of self-confidence. Skills, experience, and opportunities can all be learned and discovered. However, without self-confidence, none of those things will have the impact they otherwise could have. Unfortunately, many men lack the self-confidence that is required to achieve the success they crave. Instead, they are held back by a strong sense of self-doubt. The stronger a person's self-doubt, the harder it will be for them to achieve any real or significant success in their life.

Some symptoms of self-doubt are easy to identify, making it easy to face and overcome. However, some symptoms are more subtle, surviving in forms that are hard to detect, like cancer growing silently within. This chapter will discuss some of the most common symptoms of self-doubt, exploring the impact they can have on your life if they are allowed to exist unchecked. Additionally, this chapter will provide some easy and effective methods for overcoming self-doubt, thereby enabling you to achieve the success necessary to transform your life into that of an Alpha Male.

Common Signs of Self-Doubt

Many signs of self-doubt are obvious and easy to spot. If you constantly claim to be unable to do a certain thing, such as attract a woman or nail a job interview, then it is clear that you have serious doubts regarding your abilities in those areas. However, other symptoms of self-doubt can be harder to identify as they are disguised as rational concerns. For example, you might express self-doubt in such a way as to make the goal itself seem unreasonably hard. Instead of claiming to be bad at attracting a woman, you might use the excuse that the woman you are interested in hasn't shown any sign of being interested in you, or that she might not be looking for a relationship. Similarly, instead of putting the focus on your lack of confidence when trying to land the job of your dreams, you might focus on the fact that you don't have all the qualifications the position requires, or you might claim that your lack of experience stands against you. While these reasons may appear logical and rational, they are, in fact, symptoms of self-doubt. After all, when you have total confidence in your ability to overcome any obstacle, such issues won't be a deterrent. Instead, they will be a challenge you will happily accept.

Whether obvious or subtle, all forms of self-doubt serve to do one thing: undermine your chances of success. Therefore, you must take the time to assess your life and discover any self-doubt that might be lurking deep in your heart and mind. Identifying your self-doubts is the first step in your battle against those things that are keeping you from realizing your full potential. The following is a basic checklist outlining several of the more common signs of self-doubt. If you identify with most or all of these items, then self-doubt is a very real problem for you, one that needs to be addressed quickly and definitively.

1. You tend to hesitate about starting a new project, fearing you might not be able to complete it.

2. You lack the desire to step outside your comfort zone, even when the rewards are high.

3. You accept positions in life that are less than what you truly desire.

4. You agree with the negative things people say about you.

5. You fixate on your past failures, seeing them as signs of your inability to succeed.

6. It is hard for you to get motivated in the morning.

7. You envy the success of others.

8. You see your dreams as an escape rather than as a vision for what could be.

9. You feel self-conscious when working with others.

10. You constantly fear that you will lose what you have because of your inadequacies.

How Self-Doubt Affects You

In the end, if you recognized most or all of those elements as being a part of your life experience, you suffer from a high level of self-doubt. Now that you have recognized its existence, the next step is to understand how this self-doubt affects you. When you realize the damage that self-doubt is causing, it will serve as motivation for you to take a stand and eliminate self-doubt once and for all. The following are the three main negative impacts that self-doubt is having on your life:

- **A Lack of Drive:** Science has proven that life is all about energy. That said, there are two main charges of energy, positive and negative. When you have positive energy, you will experience positive effects, such as motivation, desire, and confidence. However, when you have negative energy, you will experience negative effects, such as a lack of drive. Thus, if you find that you lack inspiration, whether in terms of starting a new project, finding a new job, or just getting out of bed in the morning, you are suffering from the effects of self-doubt. This lack of drive can seem like a simple lack of energy at first, but what it really points to is a fear of failure. Only when self-doubt is removed can you restore your drive, thereby giving you the energy to chase your dreams.

- **A Lack of Fulfillment:** Self-doubt will often cause you to accept less than your dreams. This can come in the form of settling for a cheap car rather than the one you really want, a tiny house instead of the one you wish you had, or a job that pays the bills instead of one that brings meaning and fulfillment to your life.

- **A Lack of Success:** As mentioned before, self-confidence is one of the main ingredients in the recipe for success. That said, a lack of self-confidence will keep you from achieving success, because you will never take the first step in a journey you aren't confident of finishing. Therefore, you will take fewer and fewer chances in life, meaning that you achieve fewer and fewer successes. This lack of success is self-perpetuating. The fewer successes you have, the stronger your self-doubt will become, further hindering your chances of success down the road.

Easy and Effective Methods for Overcoming Self-Doubt

Fortunately, the methods for overcoming self-doubt are relatively simple, and easy to incorporate into your daily life. Furthermore, the methods presented in this chapter for overcoming self-doubt are highly effective, offering immediate results that will be noticeable to you and those close to you. The following are five of the easiest and most effective methods for overcoming self-doubt in all of its forms:

- **Eliminate Negative Influences:** If you take the time to ask yourself where your self-doubt comes from, you might be surprised at the answer. Often, self-doubt doesn't come from within, but from your environment. When you spend time surrounded by negative people, you will only hear negative thoughts and ideas. They will talk about how life is unfair, how any real success is impossible, and how trying to achieve your dreams will only end up in failure and despair. The more you hear this kind of talk is, the more you will begin to accept it as fact. Therefore, the first step to eliminating self-doubt is to eliminate its source, namely the negative people in your life.

- **Surround yourself with Positivity:** Once you remove the negative influences from your life, the next step is to replace them with positive influences. Try to surround yourself with successful people. Such people will have a more positive outlook on life, and that positivity will rub off on you, reprogramming your mind and eliminating the self-doubt that robs you of success. The more positivity you hear, the stronger your self-confidence will become.

- **Exercise:** One of the most ignored elements of self-doubt is its physiological causes. A lack of energy, whether physical, emotional, or mental, will often produce a sense of depression and lethargy, leading to a lack of motivation and, thus, a lack of success. Therefore, to break that cycle, you must increase your overall energy. The best way for this is to engage in some form of exercise that increases your heart and respiratory rates. Once the oxygen gets flowing through your body, your energy levels will increase, restoring confidence and inspiration.

- **Ignore your Past:** The most successful people are the ones who refuse to define themselves by their past. Instead, they focus on the present, taking every opportunity to improve their lives, becoming better and stronger every day. Focusing on the present will help you to let go of the past, especially any failures that could create self-doubt.

- **Turn Doubt into Desire:** Finally, recognize doubt for what it is. Sometimes self-doubt is a reaction to feeling you don't have the necessary skills or tools to tackle the task at hand. Rather than simply giving up, turn the doubt into the desire to acquire the skills or tools you need. You might need to ask for help, study up on a subject, or develop a new skill set. This is how growth works, so by turning doubt into desire you can grow as a result of every challenge you face. This will enable you to gain confidence as well as the experience you need to overcome every obstacle you face down the road.

Chapter 4: Body-Image Anxiety, and Four Ways to Overcome It

As discussed earlier, physical appearance can play a vital role when it comes to your sense of self-esteem. Body-image anxiety is on the rise among men, particularly in the West. Studies show that over the last twenty-four years the number of men with body-image anxiety has almost tripled, from fifteen percent of those surveyed to nearly forty-five percent. This means that as many as one in two men lack the confidence that a positive body image can provide, causing them higher levels of stress and lower levels of self-esteem. Fortunately, there are numerous proven techniques for eliminating body-image anxiety. This chapter will discuss the symptoms and effects of body-image anxiety, as well as the methods for overcoming it.

Common Forms of Body-image anxiety

Like any anxiety, body-image anxiety can take several different forms, each unique to the individual. The very attributes that some men envy can cause anxiety for those who possess them. This is because body image is all about perception. And, since each individual perceives their body differently, the anxiety they face will be different as well. Fortunately, the numerous types of body-image anxiety can be narrowed down to a few basic groups; the following are four of the most common types of body-image anxiety.

- **Weight:** Unsurprisingly, the most common of all body image anxieties is that of weight. As many as fifty percent of men feel that their weight undermines their value in the eyes of others. While extra weight and a large waist make up most of the numbers in terms of men who are self-conscious about their appearance, skinny men have also been found to suffer from body image-anxiety. Thus, it seems that the overall goal is to find that happy medium that represents strength and wellbeing. Anything else, one way or the other, results in anxiety and low self-esteem.

- **Height:** The second body image issue most men struggle with is height. Again, while short men envy the tall, most tall men suffer from their own anxieties. Stranger still, many men of average height feel that their height makes them blend in with the crowd, making them less impressive than their taller or even shorter counterparts. In the end, it seems that few men are satisfied with their height, wishing it were different in one direction or the other.

- **Muscle Tone:** This is the one area where the anxiety is easier to pinpoint, as it only goes in one direction. No man ever woke up and wished they had less muscle tone. Instead, all anxiety issues in this area come from men who feel inferior in terms of their muscular appearance. Although this might seem an easy issue to fix, one that requires little more than a gym membership, the truth of the matter is that body types are quite different, meaning that not all men can gain muscle tone simply by lifting weights.

- **Penis Size:** The final issue that causes many men body-image anxiety is that of penis size. In one survey, eighteen percent of men questioned said they were unhappy with their penis size. While the specific reasons for dissatisfaction varied, almost one in five men claimed to feel self-conscious about their penis size.

Common Effects of Body-image anxiety

Anxiety of any kind can lead to a lack of success as a result of avoiding opportunities because of one's low self-esteem. Additionally, body-image anxiety can lead to several health issues, all stemming from an individual's urgent desire to change their physical appearance. Some of the more common effects of body-image anxiety include:

- **Isolation:** Any time a man feels anxious about his physical appearance, he is more likely to avoid social contact. Isolation can lead to loneliness, depression, and an ever-growing sense of self-loathing. In more extreme cases, this can lead to thoughts and even acts of self-harm or suicide.

- **Low Self-Esteem:** As with any anxiety, self-esteem is significantly impacted when a man is self-conscious about his body image. He may begin to associate his body image with failures he experiences in life, including failed relationships, loss of employment, or a general sense of dissatisfaction with life. Since some body-image issues are hard to change, this can cause a person to feel helpless in terms of ever hoping to improve their life in any significant way.

- **Health Issues:** When a person struggles to gain or lose weight, they will often turn to supplements for help. Unfortunately, this can lead to health issues, especially when the supplements are not taken as directed, or when they are combined with others in an attempt to speed up the process. Abuse of diet pills, muscle-building compounds, and the like can lead to serious health issues, including death. Any sudden and unnatural increase or decrease in weight can impact a person's organs, causing such things as heart disease, kidney failure, and even diabetes.

- **Eating Disorders:** An all too common consequence of body-image anxiety is eating disorders. These can range from starvation diets in an attempt to lose weight to overeating in an attempt to gain weight. If a man is unable to lose weight, he may resign himself to remaining overweight, thereby becoming depressed and turning to food for comfort. Not only will this make his body-image anxiety worse, but it will also lead to potential health issues as well as depression.

Common Benefits of a Positive Body Image

When a man has a positive sense of his body image, things are quite different in terms of his overall health and wellbeing. The better a man feels about his appearance, the better he feels about himself all around. This leads to a stronger sense of self-esteem, which leads to a greater amount of self-confidence, which leads to more success in life overall. Some of the common benefits of a positive body image include:

- **Higher Levels of Self-Esteem:** When a person feels good about how they look, it increases their sense of self-worth, which inspires greater self-confidence. This translates into a better social life, better relationships with women, and even a greater chance of being satisfied in their job. The confidence that comes from feeling good about how you look translates into success in virtually every area of your life.

- **Better Health:** Another common benefit of a positive body image is better health. In a way, this can be likened to how a man treats his car. If he hates his car, the chances are he won't invest the time or energy keeping it clean and waxed and properly maintained. If he loves his car, he will keep it clean and shiny, putting the best gas in the tank and sparing no expense on parts. This is precisely how a man will treat his body. When he loves his body, he will exercise more, eat better foods, and take more time grooming. All of this increases his appearance and health, which in turn increases his confidence and overall sense of self.

Four Ways to Overcome Body-Image Anxiety for Good

While some aspects of body image are controllable, such as your appearance in terms of grooming or your general weight, others are less changeable, such as your height. Fortunately, changing your body image has more to do with your perception than it does with your actual body. You can feel good about yourself without altering your height, weight, or even muscle tone. The trick is to eliminate the negative narrative and replace it with a sense of self-worth that makes you feel good about yourself once again. The following are four ways to overcome body-image anxiety for good:

- **Eliminate the Myth of "Perfection":** One of the chief reasons people, both men, and women, develop body-image anxiety is that they feed into a notion of how their body is supposed to look. Posters, TV ads, and magazines relentlessly bombard people with images of the ideal body, making them feel inferior. The easiest way to overcome this effect is to stop seeing those images as anything but the lie they are. Perfection is a myth, pure and simple. And the images in those ads are usually airbrushed and enhanced to achieve visual perfection, anyway, meaning that they are a total lie aimed at getting you to buy a product or membership.

- **Play to your Strengths:** Sure, you might wish you were taller, or shorter, or had more hair or less hair. You might point to half a dozen things you wish were different about your appearance. That doesn't mean there aren't at least half a dozen things to be proud of. No one would ever criticize a pitcher on a baseball team for his low batting average. Nor would they expect the first baseman to get up on the mound and strike out the next batter. In baseball, as in any sport, each player focuses on their strengths to be their best. That is the trick to improving your body image. Find your best physical features and enhance them. You might have great hair, eyes, or skin. Draw attention to these things by making them what people see first. Choose clothes that make you look good, thereby giving you greater confidence. Don't focus on what you can't change; instead, focus on what works and make the most of those things.

- **Take Charge of Your Health:** Even if you can't lose or gain the exact amount of weight you want, that doesn't mean you should give up altogether. Living a healthier life will be better, no matter what. When you take the time to exercise and eat right, your body image will improve. Again, it's not about being perfect; it's about being the perfect you. As you take better care of your body, your body will perform better, and that will increase your body image exponentially.

- **Stop Comparing Yourself to Others:** Finally, you must stop comparing yourself to others. Sure, there will be other men who have better muscle tone, are the right height, the right shape, and whatever. Good for them. Don't compare yourself to them, though. Instead, recognize that your body is unique. Appreciate what you have and make the most of it. That is the key to self-esteem. It's not about being better than everyone else; it's about being the best that you can be.

Chapter 5: Five Ways to Boost Your Self-Esteem NOW

As already mentioned, self-esteem is the foundation on which any success is built. No matter what type of success you crave, your chances of success are in direct proportion to your self-esteem. When your sense of self-worth is high, your chances of realizing your ambitions will also be high; when your sense of self-esteem is low, your chances of successfully turning dreams into reality will be equally low. Therefore, before you take any action toward achieving your life goals, you must start building your sense of self-esteem. The process of building self-esteem is a gradual one, much like building muscle tone or losing weight. Fortunately, as long as you are willing to put in a little time and effort every day, the road to building high levels of self-esteem will be an easy one to travel. This chapter will discuss five of the most effective methods for giving your self-esteem the boost it so desperately needs. Once you implement these five methods into your daily routine, you will begin to notice a stronger sense of self-worth, which will increase your sense of self-confidence, thereby enabling you to tackle any challenge or pursue any goal imaginable with the best chances of success.

Live Healthy

The first thing to realize is that your mental health and wellbeing are directly connected to your physical health and wellbeing. In fact, a person's weight can often tell you the exact condition of their mind. When a person is overweight and unhealthy, their mind will be sluggish, often full of doubt and generally lacking the self-esteem necessary for achieving their life goals and ambitions. However, when a person is in good physical shape, their mind will tend to be sharper, and their self-esteem will be stronger, providing them with the confidence and peace of mind needed to tackle any challenge that comes their way effectively, thus placing them in charge of their life. Therefore, the first step toward developing high self-esteem is to get your physical health and wellbeing sorted out.

Food plays a bigger role in an individual's mental wellbeing than most people realize. Just as unhealthy foods can add unwanted pounds to your waistline, as well as clogging your arteries and creating all sorts of conditions that undermine your physical health, so too, they can have the very same impact on your mental health. Food is fuel, and your mind needs fuel to function just as much as your body does. Thus, when your diet consists of junk fuel, not only will your body suffer, but your mind will suffer as well. Depression, sluggish thinking, and an overall negative mindset go hand in hand with a diet filled with unhealthy foods. Therefore, the first thing you need to do is to replace processed foods with natural foods such as fruit and vegetables.

Additionally, make sure you eat foods rich in minerals and protein, such as eggs, fresh fish, and chicken. Get rid of sugary drinks such as soda and start drinking more water. Milk is another good choice as it contains plenty of vitamins and nutrients and has been proven to be one of the best liquids for keeping your body hydrated.

The next step to developing a healthy lifestyle is to exercise regularly. This doesn't necessarily mean you have to go out and get a gym membership today; exercise can be done at home with little to no extra gear required. Yoga, for example, is a perfect regimen to improve your heart and respiratory rates. As these rates improve, so too will your mental health and wellbeing. This will give you better clarity of mind, better memory, and an overall healthier sense of self-worth. Running is another good exercise that can boost your blood flow, thereby improving your mental performance as well as your sense of self-esteem. Starting with these exercises will get you moving in the right direction, increasing your sense of accomplishment as well as your motivation to take things to the next level.

Develop Mindfulness

The second method for giving your self-esteem an immediate boost is to develop mindfulness. This can tend to sound very Zen, and it's true that the Zen tradition is heavily steeped in mindfulness. However, you don't have to be spiritual or in search of meaning to achieve the mindfulness that you need for higher levels of self-esteem. Instead, you simply have to take the time to better understand your mind and how it works.

The best way to do this is to take time every day to sit down and be alone with your thoughts. Explore your mind, seeing and hearing all the thoughts, ideas, images, and sounds that it contains. As soon as you see an image, hear a thought, or grasp an idea, take the time to consider its meaning carefully. Where did it come from? Is it positive or negative? Any negative thought or image needs to be addressed right away as those can significantly undermine your self-esteem. Sometimes these will be the result of negative words spoken by others. Someone may have told you that a plan or idea is impossible, or that you don't have what it takes to accomplish your goals. Such thoughts need to be seen for what they are, namely the negativity of others. Once you realize that they don't actually belong to your mind, you can release them and the negativity they contain. What are left are the hopes, ambitions, and positive thoughts that will boost your self-esteem, thereby giving you the confidence necessary to achieve your goals.

Improve Your Image

The next step toward developing high levels of self-esteem is to improve your image. Although your image is something you don't see from within, the more confident you are in your appearance, the higher your sense of self-esteem will be. Therefore, this is an absolutely vital element to developing the highest levels of self-esteem, those fit for an Alpha Male.

The first area to tackle is your wardrobe. If your closet is full of uninspiring clothes, then not only will your image fail to impress others, it will fail to create high levels of self-esteem. Therefore, take the time to go through your closet and weed out all the clothes that are mediocre in style and appearance. Once you have made the space, you can go shopping for the clothes that will give your appearance the boost it needs. While loose-fitting clothes are good for sitting on the sofa, they aren't good for anything else. Therefore, fill your closet with clothes that fit well. A tailor-made shirt can make all the difference when it comes to making that all-important first impression. Pants that are the right length and fit well will help you not only look like the proverbial million dollars; they will help you feel that way, especially when you see people taking notice of you.

The next area to tackle is grooming. Always take the time to keep your fingernails and toenails neatly trimmed. Although you might be the only one to see your toes, by taking the time and effort to keep them trimmed, you are sending the message that you are worth the extra attention, and this will help boost your self-esteem. Additionally, taking the extra time and effort to make your hair look its best is vital. If you have a ten-dollar haircut you are telling yourself and everyone else that you are only worth ten dollars. However, when you spend the cash on a haircut that is tailor-made to your face, as well as the product to keep it looking its best, you are telling the world that you are worth the extra time and expense. This will make all the difference in how you feel when you step through the door into the world outside.

Manage Your Goals

When it comes to keeping your self-esteem strong and healthy, few things are as vital as a sense of accomplishment. If you struggle to achieve your goals or to make measurable progress toward fulfilling your dreams, then your self-esteem will suffer. However, when you achieve goals daily and can track your progress toward realizing the final goals, then your self-esteem will remain strong and vibrant. Fortunately, this comes down to one simple concept, that of managing your goals.

The first step toward effective goal management is to break down large goals into smaller, more achievable ones. This can keep you from feeling overwhelmed by larger projects or tasks that will take a long time to accomplish fully. Instead of approaching a big task as a single goal, you should break it down into numerous, smaller goals. This will allow you to measure the progress you are making, as well as giving you a sense of accomplishment along the way. Furthermore, as you accomplish each smaller goal, you will maintain your motivation for getting the overall project completed, thereby keeping your self-confidence high every step of the way.

Another way to manage your goals is to keep a tight schedule. Don't let yourself fall into the trap of saying that you will get to a project when you have more time. Break down large projects into smaller, more manageable tasks and give yourself realistic deadlines for those tasks. Take the time to write down your goals daily, listing out the things you want to achieve every day. If you find you are falling behind schedule, either increase your effort or reduce your workload. The important thing is to set achievable goals and to give yourself a realistic timeframe in which to get them done. This will increase your productivity, which in turn will increase your sense of self-esteem.

Be Sociable

Finally, to nurture a healthy sense of self-esteem, you must become sociable. While time alone can be a good and healthy thing, too much time alone can lead to feelings of isolation. One of the biggest problems with isolation is that it robs you of positive interactions with other people. Such interactions are critical to build and maintain high levels of self-esteem. Therefore, you must spend time with other people who can provide the positive energy and experiences needed to improve your sense of self-worth.

Spending time with the wrong people, however, can harm your self-esteem. People who are negative in their approach to life, always pointing out the bad things, gossiping about others, or just spending all their time talking about failure should be avoided at all costs. It would be better to be alone than to be in the company of negatively minded people. When you spend time with positive people, those who talk about their dreams and how they are planning to achieve them, or who offer advice and support for you in your efforts to turn your dreams into reality, then you will gain the inspiration and motivation that their positivity creates. Therefore, make sure to spend time, not just with people but with the right people.

Part Two: Alpha Male Habits

Chapter 6: The Alpha Male Profile

To become an Alpha Male, the first thing you need to do is understand exactly what an Alpha Male is. Unfortunately, many of the common notions regarding the true nature of an Alpha Male are incorrect and misleading. Most images of Alphas involve men with chiseled abs and thick biceps. Although physical strength can be significant, it is not a defining aspect of what being an Alpha Male is all about.

Furthermore, many still believe that Alpha Males have to be aggressive and intimidating. Not only is this untrue, but it is also actually the opposite of what it means to be an Alpha. Therefore, before getting into the nuts and bolts of how to develop the heart and mind of an Alpha Male, it is vital to define what this term truly means. This chapter will reveal the profile of an Alpha Male, exploring such things as the behavior, mindset, and lifestyle that are necessary for achieving this coveted title. Furthermore, it will reveal some of the benefits that come from being an Alpha Male, benefits that make the effort absolutely worthwhile.

The Language of Alphas

The first thing that separates Alpha Males from all others is the language they speak. This isn't about whether you speak English, Japanese or French; it is a different language, one that reveals the heart and mind of the Alpha Male. This language has its own tone, structure, and content, and when it is spoken, it commands the attention and respect of all who hear it.

The tone of the Alpha Male language is always confident. As such, it is neither submissive nor overbearing. A big misconception is that as an Alpha, you must always speak in a raised voice, using your proverbial "outside" voice even when indoors. This isn't the true tone of an Alpha. Instead, an Alpha Male speaks in an authoritative tone, one that is strong without being overbearing, and caring without being weak. It is neither too fast nor too slow, but deliberate and measured in its rhythm. When an Alpha Male speaks, others listen because they want to, not because they are forced to. This is one way in which an Alpha Male commands the respect of those around him.

The structure of the Alpha Male language is positive. Rather than being filled with uncertainty, it is direct and assertive. An Alpha Male will never ramble; instead, they will get straight to the point as quickly as possible. This doesn't mean that you have to be blunt and merciless in what you say. Instead, it means that you don't beat around the bush. If you have a point to make, make it. Don't sugarcoat it, and don't beat people over the head with it. In short, it comes down to integrity. An Alpha Male's words are always straight and true. They serve to convey his thoughts and feelings, nothing more, nothing less.

Finally, there is the content of the Alpha Male language. This is where positivity and confidence come into play. An Alpha Male will never belittle anyone else, even if they disagree with that person. Instead, they will always focus on the merits of their own convictions, allowing others to make up their own minds. Furthermore, their words will always be positive, demonstrating the Alpha's confidence and motivation regarding the situation at hand. There is no place for negativity, bullying, or surrender in the language of an Alpha Male. Instead, their words will be full of hope, assurance, and inspiration. They will always focus on the solution rather than the problem, demonstrating the fact that they are truly in charge of the situation.

Being Goal Oriented

Another vital aspect of the Alpha Male profile is that of being goal oriented. Everyone has dreams of one sort or another, including dreams of getting rich, finding the perfect job, or marrying the perfect woman. However, where most people fall short is in turning those dreams into reality. This is where goals are all-important. Goals are the tools with which a person can turn their dreams into reality. Without goals, dreams will never be realized, leaving the individual to live a life of mediocrity. Alphas are determined to realize their dreams, and they know that the only way to achieve that is to be goal oriented.

One way that an Alpha Male is goal oriented is how they take the time to carefully consider what has to happen to turn their dreams into reality. Once they have a dream, they begin planning how to achieve that dream. Creating goals to move them in the right direction is what an Alpha Male will do as soon as they have a clear idea of what their dream is. Rather than just being dreamers, Alpha Males are doers as well. They are the complete package. Not only can they imagine how their life can be better, they also establish the goals necessary to turn that vision into reality.

Another way that Alpha Males are goal-oriented is that they remain focused on their goals at all times. This is a sign of immeasurable discipline, especially in a world filled with distractions of all shapes and sizes. While others will end their day with hours of TV, games, or other distractions, Alpha Males will use that time to further their ambitions. Instead of wasting time, they invest their time, reaping the benefits of fulfilling their dreams. While Alpha Males might appear as workaholics at times, the truth is that they are simply unwilling to rest until their goals are achieved, and their lives transformed into their dreams.

Being A Leader

The Alpha Male is the top dog, the one in charge, the one that everyone else follows. Therefore, as an Alpha Male, you must be a leader.

There are many qualities to leadership, qualities that not only make a true leader stand out from the crowd but that serve to engender trust, confidence, and respect in those around them. One of the most important of all leadership qualities is that of integrity. Not only must an Alpha Male speak the truth at all times, but they must also stay true to their principles. This means that they must always make the right choice, even when that choice might be the hardest one to make. Rather than giving in to pressure from peers or even pressure from superiors, an Alpha Male will always stay true to his personal beliefs. An Alpha Male will run the risk of being fired from his job or ostracized by his friends and family rather than doing something that goes against his core values. This unwavering sense of right is what is at the very heart of a true Alpha Male.

Another vital element of being a leader is the ability to connect to others. This includes those above you, around you, and in your charge. A true Alpha Male will listen to what others have to say, taking their opinions seriously even if he doesn't agree with them. He recognizes that to get others to listen to him, he must listen to them as well. Making even the lowest person on the totem pole feel important is a trait of an Alpha Male. This means that the bullying, overbearing image of Alpha Males that is so prevalent today is about as far from the truth as you could get. A real Alpha doesn't have to threaten or bully people into submission; instead, they can assert their authority simply by showing true strength of character.

Finally, to be a good leader, you must be able to lead by example. Just because someone is in charge doesn't mean they are a good leader. A good way to tell the difference is to see whether or not the person in charge holds themselves to the same standards as they hold everyone else. Inept leaders will often use the phrase, "Do as I say, not as I do." This demonstrates a total weakness of character since it means the leader is incapable of maintaining the standards they expect of others.

In contrast, an Alpha Male will hold themselves to even higher standards than those around them. This means that they will lead by example, always putting forth a strong work ethic, a willingness to learn new skills, and the ability to adapt to changing situations. In short, they will never expect others to do what they are not willing or able to do themselves.

Benefits of Being an Alpha Male

The qualities of an Alpha Male discussed above are far from a complete list. Even so, they represent some of the most demanding and disciplined aspects a person could ever hope to achieve. This often leads to questions of whether or not the effort is worthwhile. After all, there had better be something at the end of the race to make the race worth running. Fortunately, there are many benefits to being an Alpha Male. In fact, the benefits are so numerous and so significant that they make every effort required for becoming an Alpha Male almost seem minimal in comparison.

One such benefit of being an Alpha Male is the sense of being your own person. Most people resign themselves to being a product of their environment or their opportunities. This means that they live a life largely decided for them by others. In contrast, an Alpha Male never defines himself or his potential by his surroundings. Instead, he determines his own life by following his ambitions, no matter where they may lead. This means that as an Alpha, you will never be a victim again. Your fate won't be decided by the family you were born into, or the opportunities others offer. Instead, your fate will be determined by your ambitions and your ability to realize those ambitions.

Another benefit of being an Alpha Male is the choices at your disposal. The more average a person is, the more average their choices are. Someone with mediocre ambitions will only ever achieve mediocre success. The jobs available to them will be limited in terms of fulfillment and financial gain. The women who are in "their league" will be mediocre, promising a future of modest happiness. While these can be enough for many, it is hardly the stuff dreams are made of. This is where being an Alpha Male can make all the difference. Once you develop and integrate Alpha qualities into your life, you will find your opportunities increase exponentially. Better jobs are within reach, higher income levels are there for the taking, and the woman of your dreams will want to share her life with you as she recognizes the Alpha Male within you.

Finally, when you are an Alpha Male, your perspective on life changes dramatically. While most people wake up day after day wondering what obstacles they will face in the day to come, as an Alpha Male you will wonder what opportunities await you in the day ahead. This makes every day a wonderful adventure, full of unlimited potential. Rather than dreading the future, you will eagerly anticipate it. The reason for this is that you know your ability to make things happen, so each day is an opportunity for you to make yet another dream come true. Thus, instead of life being something to be endured or tolerated, it becomes something to get excited about. Every day will be a tool that you use to turn your dreams into reality. As an Alpha Male, life's challenges don't dictate your life to you, but allow you to live it.

Chapter 7: Why Women Prefer Alphas

Although it stands to reason that women would prefer Alpha Males over any other type, there can still be a bit of confusion in this area. After all, there are plenty of books and articles devoted to the subject of women being attracted to gentle, caring men who aren't afraid to show their emotional side. This has led to many men choosing to pursue a Beta Male lifestyle in hopes of being more attractive to women. Unfortunately for them, the notion of women preferring Beta Males is completely misguided. Half of the reason is that many of the Alpha-Male traits women claim to be turned off by aren't true qualities of the Alpha Male at all. In fact, they are qualities an Alpha Male would reject. The other half of the reason is that while women want to be able to share a tender, emotional moment with their man, they don't want to have to baby him, as is often the case with Beta Males.

The reasons why women prefer Alpha Males are very simple and straightforward. This chapter will reveal several of those reasons, giving you the inside scoop on why you will attract more women when you develop your Alpha Male lifestyle.

The Primal Mind

When discussing the reasons why women prefer Alpha Males, one of the first things to consider is the biology of the situation. Humans are a species of mammals, hardwired in many ways the same as any other species in nature. This means that the emotions and impulses that drive us are primal, the very same ones that drove our cave-dwelling ancestors to make the same sorts of choices that we make today. In this light, it becomes obvious why a woman would prefer to share her life with an Alpha Male.

For one thing, Alpha Males are stronger. Again, this isn't necessarily about muscles or martial arts abilities; rather, it's about strength of character. An Alpha Male has the confidence and drive needed to achieve his goals. Therefore, he is seen as stronger than those who are timid or who lack motivation. Although what constitutes strength in the Alpha Male has evolved over the millennia, the natural attraction to strength has not, meaning that women are instinctively drawn to Alpha Males more so than to any other type.

Although the ability to achieve goals can enable an Alpha Male to achieve success and fame, the true significance of this ability is that the Alpha Male can provide security for himself and his family. This is another way in which the primal mind can be seen at work. What a woman craves is the certainty that she will always have a comfortable home, plenty of food, and all of her needs met. Since an Alpha Male is the epitome of success, both in the workplace as well as in other environments, such security is always guaranteed. Thus, just as the prehistoric woman was attracted to the male who could build a solid shelter and successfully hunt for food, so too, the modern woman is attracted to the man who can satisfy her basic needs.

Finally, there is the matter of pride. While it's likely that Alpha Males in prehistoric times would compete in feats of strength to get their position, modern-day Alphas don't have to rely on such acts any longer. Instead, having a prestigious job, a nice house, and a strong bank account provide the same bragging rights as did knocking the other males to the ground back in the day. Although such things may be seen as shallow and materialistic by some, the fact is that they all point to the financial security that triggers that primal drive. Not only is it a primal drive in Alpha Males to achieve such success, but it is also a primal drive in females to be attracted to it. No woman was ever put off by a large bank account, a big house, or a lifestyle that was too good. Instead, they are put off by the arrogance, misogyny, and abusive behavior of a Beta Male who has those things. The security and happiness that such things provide is always attractive to any woman, both ancient and modern.

Alpha Attributes That Women Love

If you haven't yet achieved the fortune that will attract a woman, never fear. Many Alpha Male attributes will attract a woman regardless of your bank account or the car you drive. However, those attributes should serve to drive you to achieve success in other areas, thereby proving that you can provide the security and happiness every woman wants.

One such attribute is that of confidence. No matter what situation an Alpha Male finds himself in, one certain thing is that he will always be confident of achieving success. Even if his life has been turned upside down by forces beyond his control, rather than mourning his losses and dreading the future, a true Alpha Male will see his condition as an opportunity to build a fresh life, one that is even better than the one he lost.

Such confidence doesn't lead to arrogance, however. Instead, it leads to cooperation and support on a level that is unmistakable. Men who sing their own praises, often at the expense of belittling others, aren't showing confidence or pride; they are showing a need for validation, something that reflects insecurity and anxiety. Alpha Males will share their confidence with others, offering support, guidance, and even help to others who are struggling to achieve their goals. Such confidence brings with it a sense of compassion that resonates with women. This is one of those areas of confusion regarding true Alpha Male qualities. Showing compassion isn't a Beta Male trait, rather it is a trait of someone who isn't afraid of being shown up and who craves success, both for himself as well as for those around him. In short, compassion is very much a trait of an Alpha Male.

Another Alpha Male trait that draws in women is that of dominance. Herein is another example of misunderstanding the true nature of the Alpha-Male mindset. Dominance doesn't mean that you rise to the top by stepping on those around you. Instead, it is a matter of energy. When you crave success like an Alpha Male, you put in your best performance every time you take on a challenge. This can be in any area at all, including projects at work, projects at home, or even a fun day out with friends and loved ones. A simple game of darts, for example, will bring out the competitive nature of an Alpha Male. Even though it's just a game, one that won't change anyone's life in any way, shape, or form, an Alpha Male will put every effort into winning. His energy and commitment will make him stand out, dominating those around him. The best part is that even if he doesn't win, not only will his exceptional efforts be recognized, his graciousness in defeat will also make him stand out head and shoulders above the rest. It's not that he enjoys losing as such. Rather, it shows that he is strong enough to share in another person's success.

What Alpha Males Bring to a Relationship

While a show of financial security and reliable attributes will go a long way to attracting a woman, these may not prove enough to keep her by your side once you win her over. To achieve that goal, the goal of keeping a woman for the long term, you need to master the traits that make a relationship work. Fortunately, the same traits that ensure an Alpha Male success in other areas of life will also ensure success in the area of long-term relationships. Therefore, while Beta Males will struggle to keep a woman interested, Alphas will keep a woman by their side for as long as they choose.

One of the most important Alpha Male qualities when it comes to making a relationship work is that of being direct. While women might like a bit of mystery, they don't like to play games when it comes to starting a relationship. A mistake most men make is that they say whatever they think a woman wants to hear to get their foot in the proverbial door. Unfortunately, as time progresses, those statements are seen as deceptions, leading to conflict and failed relationships. In contrast, Alpha Males are always honest, telling a woman the truth about everything from the start. Although this truth may not be ideal, such as the Alpha Male not liking dogs while the woman is a dog lover, at least she will know upfront that there are challenges to be met. This creates trust and respect, qualities that are the very foundation of every successful and long-lasting relationship.

Another way in which the mindset of an Alpha Male is beneficial in a relationship is that it reduces and even eliminates stress on the part of the woman. One of the main causes of stress in a relationship is uncertainty. If a woman is unsure of how the man feels or what he is thinking, she can create all kinds of negative scenarios in her mind that cause untold stress and anxiety. An Alpha Male will always be direct with his thoughts and feelings, removing any uncertainty and the stress and anxiety such uncertainty can cause. This also prevents a woman from feeling as though she is wasting her time. Instead of putting vast amounts of time and effort into an uncertain relationship, she will know whether the relationship has a future by the things the Alpha Male says and does.

Finally, the confidence of an Alpha Male will go a long way toward creating a healthy and vibrant relationship on all levels. One thing that this confidence will do is enable an Alpha to open up to his partner. This prevents her from feeling shut out, as is the case with so many "macho" men who are, in fact, Beta in nature. Since an Alpha is unafraid of rejection, he will be completely willing to share his feelings on any matter. This is the tender side of a man that is often wrongly associated with Beta Males.

This confidence will also enable an Alpha to step out of his comfort zone. There will be a time in any relationship where the woman wants to do something that the man simply does not want to do. While Betas will either refuse to participate or find excuses that allow them to avoid the issue, Alphas will gladly, if reluctantly, indulge their partner in an activity that would bring other men to their knees. Going to a chick flick, for example, is something that an Alpha might not want to do, but he will gladly do it to make his woman happy. He won't be concerned about who sees him entering or leaving the theater, and he won't have to bring a chain saw to prove he is still a man. He will accompany his lady with pride and confidence, making him stand out in a way most men only ever dream of.

Why You Should Go the Alpha Way

In the end, if you want to both attract and keep the woman of your dreams, there is only one way to go; the way of the Alpha Male. Again, this isn't about getting ripped with muscles to impress, nor is it about being tough and macho. The trick is to be a true Alpha, someone full of confidence and integrity, qualities that will enable you to please any woman for any length of time. As well as being qualities that benefit the woman, the Alpha qualities of confidence and integrity will also keep you happy as well.

One way that confidence can make you happy in terms of a relationship is that it will keep you from staying in a relationship that makes you miserable. There are times when the woman of your dreams may turn out to actually be the stuff of nightmares. If you lack the confidence to find another, better relationship, you may resign yourself to being miserable in lieu of being alone. However, when you possess the confidence of an Alpha Male, you know that you not only deserve better but that you are capable of finding better. This will allow you to leave a toxic relationship before it can negatively affect your life.

Another way that confidence will benefit you is that you will never be afraid of losing the woman of your dreams to another man.

Sometimes even a Beta Male can do the right things and say the right words to win the prize. However, such a prize will only cause him misery down the road as he will always be jealous and suspicious of any other man. When you have the confidence of an Alpha Male, you will feel secure in the fact that the woman of your dreams will never leave your side. No man will be able to compete with you and win her affections. This will make every day with her one to be celebrated, not feared.

Chapter 8: Alpha Male Habit #1: Confidence

The key to developing any kind of lifestyle is to develop the right habits. This is evident even in terms of bad lifestyles, where habits such as eating fast food and not getting exercise lead to poor health, low self-esteem, and a mediocre life at best. In contrast, when you create positive, strong habits, you will create a positive and strong lifestyle. This applies to even the strongest and most positive of lifestyles, namely that of the Alpha Male. Since confidence is the foundation on which the Alpha Male lifestyle is built, the first habit you need to form is that of practicing confidence. This chapter will discuss the things to avoid when creating this habit, such as the many false faces of confidence that are commonly mistaken as Alpha Male qualities. Additionally, you will be given specific actions to take daily that will make confidence a natural part of your behavior. Finally, some of the benefits of having confidence in your life will be presented, giving you extra motivation for getting started on developing your Alpha Male lifestyle.

False Faces of Confidence

It may seem repetitive to keep referring to the qualities most people mistakenly associate with being an Alpha Male, but the truth of the matter is that these qualities can be devastating to anyone who is trying to develop a true Alpha Male lifestyle. Therefore, before you begin learning the true signs of confidence and the steps needed to develop them, it is vital that you recognize the false faces of confidence so that you can avoid them at all costs. The following are some of the most common false faces of confidence:

- **Bullying People:** The behavior of a bully may appear as confident, but you should recognize that it is actually quite cowardly, because a bully invariably picks on someone they think weaker than themselves.

- **Bragging:** While bragging may appear confident, it is, in fact, a sign that a person needs validation. Someone who is truly confident won't have to put themselves in the spotlight the way a braggart does. Instead, they are confident of their abilities regardless of what others may say. They are happy to remain silent about their successes; they never have to seek praise or recognition.

- **Gossiping:** Like bullying, gossiping is when one person denigrates another, although in this case, it's behind their back. No person with self-confidence would engage in this behavior; putting other people down to look good is just another form of cowardice.

Habits of Insecure People

In addition to false faces of confidence, some habits must absolutely be avoided to build an Alpha Male lifestyle. These habits are those caused by a lack of self-esteem and self-confidence. While some may seem harmless enough, if allowed to continue, they will undermine your efforts at creating the life of your dreams. Some common habits of insecure people include the following:

- **Needing Constant Validation:** One of the most tell-tale signs of insecurity is a constant need for validation. If you constantly seek approval, recognition, or the proverbial pat on the back, you lack the self-esteem of an Alpha Male. Only when you quit this habit can you begin to form those that will give you the confidence you desire.

- **Lack of Grooming:** One thing that builds confidence is taking care of your physical appearance. Thus, when you stop taking care of such things as your hair, skin, and other basic elements, you demonstrate a low sense of self-esteem. Never let yourself fall into the habit of poor personal grooming.

- **Apathy:** When someone has confidence, they tend to seek out opportunities, eagerly chasing anything that could potentially help them create the life of their dreams. Alternatively, someone lacking confidence will wait for things to happen. This is a sign they are waiting to be rescued, meaning they require a savior figure to be free. Since an Alpha Male is his own savior figure, apathy has no place in the Alpha Male lifestyle.

- **Avoiding Eye Contact:** Anyone who avoids eye contact is either a liar or someone with a complete lack of self-confidence. Few things appear as submissive as being unable to maintain healthy eye contact with another person.

- **Constantly Apologizing:** It is one thing to apologize for stepping on a person's foot, or for making a mistake. It's quite something else to apologize for everything, even things that aren't your fault in any way, shape, or form. This is nothing short of an attempt to make everyone else happy at your own expense. Again, not something an Alpha Male would ever do.

Signs of True Confidence

Now that you have an idea of some of the common habits of insecure people, it's time to take a look at the signs of true confidence. These are the habits that any Alpha Male will practice every day, making them stand out from the rest of the crowd. Some signs of true confidence include:

- **Strong Body Language:** Such things as good posture, uncrossed arms, a wide stance, and a powerful stride reflect confidence. All of these are examples of strong body language, something that engenders respect and confidence in those around you. Being able to maintain eye contact with another person is another example.

- **Being well-groomed:** When you invest the time, effort, and money into taking care of your body, you tell the rest of the world that you are worth it. This not only makes you more attractive to those you interact with, but it also demonstrates the fact that you possess high levels of self-confidence.

- **Being well dressed:** In addition to taking the time and effort to care for your skin, hair, and overall physical self, it is vital that you put the same time and effort into the clothes you wear. Wearing average clothes will make you look average; when you dress in clothes that fit well, that are stylish, and that stand out, you send the message that you are confident and capable.

- **Being Supportive:** Whether it's lending an ear, a shoulder to cry on, or actual assistance for someone who's having a hard time, being supportive is a sign that you are a true Alpha Male. This is because Alphas know they have enough ability to not only ensure their own success but to help others achieve success as well. A truly confident man doesn't need to put others down to feel good about himself. Instead, he takes pride and satisfaction in raising others up.

- **Integrity:** Saying what you mean and keeping the promises you make are signs of true confidence. Alpha Males will not tell people only what they want to hear, nor will they make promises they can't keep. Furthermore, they will have a code of conduct that they keep regardless of circumstances. An Alpha Male will never compromise his values.

Steps to Building Confidence

While you may already have some of these positive habits in your life, others may need to be developed from scratch. Fortunately, the process of developing any habit is fairly easy and straight forward. The trick is to find a behavior that embodies the habit and to practice that behavior daily. Eventually, the behavior will become second nature, making it and its qualities a part of your everyday life. The following are some behaviors to practice to develop the habit of confidence:

- **Improve your Appearance:** As mentioned earlier, appearance is a huge part of self-confidence. This goes for grooming as well as the clothes you wear. Therefore, the first step to developing confidence is to go through your closet and get rid of all the clothes that are old, worn, or ordinary. Replace them with clothes that make you look and feel your best.

  Additionally, change your haircut. Stop going to the ten-dollar place and spend the cash for a proper stylist to give you the makeover you deserve. Give yourself thirty days to achieve these goals of improving your personal appearance.

- **Become Sociable:** Anyone who has struggled with insecurity will know how hard it can be to interact with strangers. However, the only way to build confidence is to face your fears. Therefore, the next step is to begin interacting with people regularly. Strike up conversations with baristas or cashiers, asking about their day. Maintain eye contact with them as you do, ensuring you connect with them in a meaningful way. Take thirty days to develop this skill, starting slowly but being strong in the end.

- **Take Charge of your Finances:** One of the main causes of low self-esteem is financial insecurity. While you may not be able to go out and double your income right away, you can take the time to ensure you eliminate bad spending habits. Take thirty days to go over your spending habits and eliminate all the unnecessary spending that results in you struggling financially. This will also provide the necessary cash for such things as better hairstyle and better clothes.

- **Take Charge of your Job:** Unless you are one of a very small minority, the chances are you are unhappy with your job in some way. Rather than accepting the situation, take the next thirty days to improve it. Either look for ways to improve the job you have or start looking for another job altogether. Freshen your resume and use your newly developed skills in socializing and looking your best to get a job that makes you happy as well as pays the bills.

- **Surround yourself with Friends:** One habit many people fall into is that of becoming isolated. This can significantly undermine a person's sense of self-esteem. Therefore, over the next thirty days, spend good quality time with those people who make you feel loved and appreciated. Invite them over for dinner or go out on the town. As long as you surround yourself with love and positivity, your confidence will continue to grow.

- **Find your Faith:** Every person needs a belief system that they can fall back on when times are hard, and to which they can aspire for self-betterment. This doesn't mean you have to choose a religion as such; rather, it means you should sit down and decide what your beliefs are. Furthermore, take the time to feel good about all the things you have. Be grateful for the people in your life, your opportunities, and even your desire to do better. In short, take the next thirty days to discover and write down the things that truly matter to you.

Impact of Confidence on Your Life

There is almost no end to the benefits that high levels of self-confidence can bring to your life. However, simply saying that may not be enough to keep you motivated when it comes to forming the habits needed to increase self-confidence. Instead, you might need a solid reward in sight, a prize to keep your eyes on to keep you moving in the right direction. The following are a few examples of the prizes that await someone with high self-confidence:

- **Increased Attractiveness:** Habits such as maintaining eye contact, dressing and grooming for success, and the like do more than just increase your sense of confidence. They serve to make you more attractive to others. Therefore, as you develop these habits, you will make yourself more desirable in the eyes of others. This includes women, potential employers, landlords, salespeople, and others who might hold sway over your future success. The confidence you exude when interacting with these people will often serve to put you closer to the life of your dreams.

- **Increased Opportunity:** One thing that confidence allows you to do is to step outside your comfort zone. This will enable you to find opportunities that might not have been available to you otherwise. The more opportunities you create, the more likely you are to achieve the success you both desire and deserve.

- **Better Choices:** When you struggle with insecurity, you tend to make decisions out of fear rather than out of desire. You might settle for a job that you know you can do instead of pursuing the job of your dreams. Likewise, you might settle for a woman that makes you "happy enough" instead of chasing the one that will make every day feel like Christmas. However, when you have high levels of confidence, you will make better choices, and those choices will help you to create the life of your dreams.

Chapter 9: Alpha Male Habit #2: Persistence

One of the biggest misconceptions regarding success is that it should somehow be instantaneous. In a world of immediate gratification, from fast food to next-day delivery, people have become accustomed to getting what they want without delay. If you take the time to observe the situation, you will notice a sinister truth; most things that can be achieved instantly aren't worth achieving. Take food, for example; any food that can be prepared in five minutes or less will not be the kind of food you write home about. On the other hand, a meal for which you had to wait half an hour or more was usually well worth the wait.

This is true in all areas of life, not just food. Any significant success will take time to achieve. Unfortunately, this is where most people fail. They don't have the single quality necessary to achieve the worthwhile results: persistence. Alpha Males, by contrast, possess the persistence needed to achieve those lofty goals, the ones that lead to life-changing success. This chapter will discuss some of the ways in which persistence pays off, as well as ways to develop the habit of being persistent.

Avoiding the Easy Path

Sometimes you will be faced with two choices at the most critical junctures in your life. The first choice is the easy choice, the one that requires the least amount of time, effort, and resources on your part. This is the choice that promises instant gratification. The other choice is the hard choice, the one that demands greater amounts of time, energy and resources to see the finished result. Although this choice proves more demanding in every way, it always promises to deliver results that are worth the extra investment. This is why the harder choice is often referred to as the "right choice" by Alpha Males.

When you make the harder choice, two things happen. First, you protect yourself from inferior results. When you turn away from the drive-in window at the fast-food restaurant, you protect yourself from the processed meats, fatty oils, and foods heavy in starch and salt that such places offer. In other words, you protect your body from excess weight, clogged arteries, and high blood pressure. No amount of time saved is worth that cost.

The second thing that happens when you make the harder choice is that you set yourself up for greater success. Sure, going to a good restaurant that serves freshly prepared food might cost more, and it will definitely take more time to get your food, but the finished product will be infinitely better than the poison you would be eating out of a paper bag. Your body and mind will be healthier and happier, improving your very quality of life. Eventually, as an Alpha Male, you will begin to see the harder choice as usually being the more attractive one.

How Persistence Turns the Tables

The idea of better results requiring greater effort can be seen in all areas of life. One such area is that of sculpting your body. Given a choice between going to the gym and staying home to watch TV, most people choose the easier option. The result is that the average person tends to be overweight, short of energy, and ultimately low on self-esteem. Those who choose to go to the gym wind up with higher levels of physical health, mental health, and general sense of wellbeing, which lead ultimately to greater self-esteem.

Furthermore, the person who goes to the gym has the option of going for perhaps twenty minutes a day three times a week, or for an hour a day five times a week. Again, the individual who makes the harder choice will gain the best results. In the end, the choice between easy and hard is always present. The more you choose the hard road, the better your outcome will inevitably be.

Another way that persistence can pay off is by wearing down resistance. Take, for example, the case of someone chasing after the job of their dreams. At first, they may not get the job, as it might go to someone with more experience, or as is so often the case, who knows someone on the inside. Most people would see that first shot as having been their one chance for success and walk away resigned to never getting that job. In contrast, an Alpha Male will persist in his efforts, sending in application after application, going on interview after interview. Eventually, the resistance will be broken, and the persistence will win the day. The Alpha Male realizes one simple secret, namely the fact that the result is what counts, not the time or effort it takes to achieve the result.

Stone is much harder than water, so rain will bounce off of a stone wall without leaving a trace. However, if stone is exposed to a constant water source, it will eventually wear away. The Grand Canyon, one of the world's largest valleys, was created by a river gradually eating away at the stone. This is one of nature's examples of how persistence can win out against all the odds.

What Persistence Says About A Man

Persistence is a quality that can easily be seen by others, and it says a lot about the man being observed. One thing persistence says about a man is that he is willing to do whatever it takes to achieve his goals. This means that he is not addicted to immediate gratification nor inclined to settle for lesser victories. Instead, he is dedicated to creating the very best results possible.

Another thing persistence says about a man is that he isn't lazy. Only a person who is full of energy and passion can remain persistent until their goal is achieved. These attributes are very attractive, not only to women but also to businessmen, bosses, and leaders of all types who are looking for the best men to bring onto their team. Thus, when an Alpha Male uses his persistence to achieve his goals, he draws attention to himself, the type of attention that will open all sorts of doors and put countless opportunities within his reach.

Finally, when a man is persistent, he demonstrates the fact that he knows what he wants. This means that his life is already on a trajectory toward success. Alpha Males have a strong sense of what they want, meaning that they are moving toward a destination.

Examples of Persistence in Our World

Ironically enough, some of the technology that has led to a culture accustomed to instant gratification owes its existence to technology that took unrelenting persistence to develop. Thomas Edison went through one thousand failed attempts before discovering the design that ultimately changed the world we live in today.

Henry Ford persisted through five bankruptcies before finally establishing the Ford Motor Company.

Walt Disney persisted through multiple failed businesses before reaching his breakthrough, a breakthrough that has changed the world of entertainment forever.

Albert Einstein persisted through many years of struggle before finally realizing the theories that would revolutionize the world of science.

Dr. Seuss, the world-renowned author of children's books, was rejected twenty-seven times before finally getting his first book published.

Michael Jordan was dropped from the basketball team at his high school for not meeting expectations.

Vincent van Gogh only sold one painting in his lifetime, yet his work is considered unparalleled in the art world today.

NASA experienced twenty failures in twenty-eight attempts to send a rocket into space.

These are but a few of the many examples of people who persisted through failure and struggled to achieve their goals. The lesson to be learned is that persistence is the key to success. It doesn't matter who you are or where you come from. You can have every resource at your disposal and still suffer countless setbacks before achieving success. You may be bankrupt and without prospects, yet success lies just around the corner, waiting for you to discover it. Only when you persist will you reach the final destination, the one where all the struggle and hardship pay off. Then you can enjoy the fruits of your success: the life of your dreams.

Chapter 10: Alpha Male Habit # 3: Frame

Another critical habit to form to develop an Alpha Male mindset is that of maintaining a dominant frame. In this case, a frame is an individual's outlook on reality. It is the framework from which they perceive the world around them. Every single person operates within their own unique frame, meaning that no two people see reality in exactly the same way. Different realities can collide from time to time, creating a competition of sorts. One reality must submit to the other for both people to coexist. As an Alpha Male, you rarely want to submit to someone else's frame. Instead, you must be the one to establish the reality in which everyone else exists. This chapter will discuss the impact that controlling the frame will have on your life, as well as numerous methods for developing the ability to create and maintain a dominant frame.

The Trap of Compromise

Many traditions teach the importance of compromise, asserting that when everyone is willing to give a little in a situation, no one has to lose. This theory sounds wonderful, but it is one of the countless theories that work far better on paper than in reality. The truth of the matter is that every situation contains a certain momentum. As one person gives in to the demands of the other, they begin to move in a negative direction; despite the other person reciprocating, they continue to move in a positive direction, taking as much as they can until they are ultimately the winner. This doesn't mean that one person is good and the other bad, it is just a reflection of human nature. In fact, it reflects the hard wiring of all species; any time animals interact, one will attain dominance while the others become submissive.

This is the trap of compromise. Every time you give in to another person's demands, it not only undermines your position, but it also strengthens the position of the other person. Therefore, even the smallest concession can turn into the first step down a very slippery slope, one that will see you at the bottom while the other person is at the top. Therefore, you must never give an inch when you have a clear idea of the goal you want to achieve. Only by holding fast to your vision will you have any chance of achieving that goal. This is one way that you control the frame.

Another trap of compromise is that every time you concede to accommodate someone else's goals or desires, you are letting them live your life. Now, rather than your time and effort leading to achieving your goals, they lead to achieving the goals of someone else. Eventually, it is as though your life is no longer yours. It's as if the other person has two lives now, or even more depending on how many people are submitting to their will. This may not happen overnight; it usually evolves over a long period. Giving an inch here and an hour there may seem small at the moment, but over time those small sacrifices add up, resulting in you sacrificing miles and years in the end. The best way to avoid this pitfall is to never compromise for anyone, ever.

Establishing Your Personal Frame

The common understanding of compromise is that the opposite of compromise is tyranny. In other words, if you are unwilling to give a little, it must mean that you intend to control everyone else. This isn't the true opposite of compromise at all. Instead, the true opposite is *independence*. When you are unwilling to sacrifice your ideals or goals for someone else's happiness, you are independent of what other people feel, do, or say. This is the face of true freedom. Therefore, to be free of the influences and controls of others, you must avoid compromise. The best way to achieve this goal is to establish your personal frame.

One of the main elements of your personal frame is your set of goals. When you have specific goals that you want to achieve, then that becomes the frame of your reality. Any action, idea, thought, or word that leads to the achievement of your goals fits into your frame. Everything else falls outside your frame, as it will likely only impede your progress, or worse, lead you away from your desired destination. Peer pressure, for example, won't affect you when you have a solid frame. While others may submit to the pressure and change their actions, you will stay the course, holding true to the values that will lead you to success.

In the end, as well as being your perception of life as a whole, your frame is your perception of your personal life. It is how you see yourself in the here and now, as well as the vision of where you see yourself in the future. It is about your actions, your beliefs, and your vision of what success truly means. In this light, creating a strong frame isn't about controlling others; instead, it is about gaining ultimate control over your own life and never allowing outside influences to take that control away.

Maintaining Your Personal Frame

Once you have established your frame, the next step is to maintain that frame at all costs. As just noted, to maintain the integrity of your frame you must avoid the trap of compromise at all costs. Another bad habit that needs to be broken to maintain your personal frame is that of being reactionary. All too often, it can seem necessary to try to convince others that your vision, values, or goals are right. However, every time you try to convince another person of your frame you are actually submitting to theirs; when you maintain your frame, you aren't worried about what others think or say. In fact, you are willing to lose support from those who don't see things your way.

It's a bit like driving a bus; as the driver, you decide the direction the bus is going. If some of the passengers don't like it, they can get off at the next stop. Those who choose to stay on are the people who agree with your direction and thus are the ones you want by your side.

This leads to a very important rule that every Alpha Male applies to their life. That rule is to gain control over your emotions. Any time a person lashes out in anger or frustration, they abandon their own frame and become consumed by the frame of another. Such outbursts only serve to reveal insecurity within the individual; insecurity born of doubt, low self-esteem, and all the other elements that are contrary to an Alpha Male's mindset. As an Alpha Male, you must maintain emotional equilibrium at all times. Always stay focused on your goals and your frame. If someone else disagrees with or challenges your frame, realize that you don't have anything to prove. By staying true to yourself, you will gain the respect of those who are truly worthwhile.

Anyone who doesn't respect your Alpha Male qualities is someone you are better off without.

For example, let's say you wanted to sell your house, and you were asking two hundred thousand dollars for it. Numerous people may come along and make counteroffers, usually for far less than the asking price. By avoiding compromise, you ensure that you achieve your success, not the success of someone else. Furthermore, you never have to get angry or frustrated with any person who makes a counteroffer. All you have to do is reject each counteroffer with dignity and respect. The fact that they don't want to spend the money you are asking for doesn't mean you are in the wrong. You aren't trying to sell your house to any particular person anyway. The truth of the matter is that it doesn't matter who buys your house. The important thing is that you sell your house and that you get the price you are asking. Eventually, a buyer will come along and agree on terms. Then *you* are the winner as you held fast to your frame, maintaining your integrity and vision every step of the way. Ironically enough, the person who will buy the house will usually be one of the people who made counteroffer after counteroffer trying to get you to compromise, thus proving that your frame was reasonable after all.

Chapter 11: Alpha Male Habit # 4: Physical Appearance

One thing that cannot be overstated is the simple fact that being an Alpha Male is about so much more than having a perfectly sculpted physique. Confidence, charm, purpose, and other similar qualities are all vital elements of the Alpha Male personality. However, none of this means that exercise and bodybuilding should be ignored or avoided. Just because they are not the be-all and end-all to being an Alpha Male, they still play a pivotal role. Therefore, one habit that is recommended for developing your Alpha Male lifestyle is to work on your physique daily. This chapter will highlight some of the more common and effective methods for creating a physical appearance that will attract the right attention from the right people.

Creating A Healthy Appearance

When it comes to creating the physical appearance of an Alpha Male, you must begin by focusing on your health. No amount of muscle tone will show through unwanted pounds around the waist or on your arms. Therefore, before going to the gym to lift weights and build those biceps, you need to achieve the ideal weight for your height and age. Since this varies from person to person, it is recommended that you either do some research online to determine your ideal weight or partner with a trainer who can guide you in the right direction.

Diet is the most important element when it comes to controlling your weight. Regardless of whether you are looking to add pounds to a skinny frame or take off pounds from a rounder frame, the foods you eat, along with the portions and times of day you eat your meals, will significantly affect your progress. Therefore, even before you begin any exercise regimen, you must get rid of all the junk foods and start eating healthy foods such as vegetables, fruits, and high-protein foods like eggs, beans, and fish. The latter are excellent sources of protein and other nutrients that can help create a healthy body weight no matter which direction you need to go. Also, drinking plenty of fluids, mostly water or milk, will help to give you the body mass needed to make all other efforts worthwhile.

Along with eating the right foods, it is recommended that you begin a regimen of daily supplements to assist you in changing your body mass. Any nutrition store or reputable gym will have plenty of vitamins, nutritional supplements, and other items that will help to burn fat, increase weight, or help you in whatever way you require. While many people shy away from supplements, they can actually make a huge difference in how soon you begin to see results. Taking fat-busting pills on their own won't get the job done. However, when combined with a healthy diet and exercise the results will be exponentially better. The trick is to not rely on any single solution; instead, implement several different efforts at the same time. This increases not only your chances of success but the very level of success you can achieve.

The third prong of your attack will take the shape of cardio workouts. Whether you are trying to lose weight or improve your body's tone, cardio workouts are essential for your progress. Combined with diet and supplements, these workouts will impact every single area of your health and wellbeing.

Integrating multiple approaches is one of two key ingredients when it comes to creating a healthy physical appearance; the second ingredient is consistency. Unless you create *the habits* of exercising, eating right, and taking nutritional supplements, you will only achieve nominal results. Even worse, those results may not last if you allow yourself to go back to the old habits that robbed you of your physical health and wellbeing in the first place. Therefore, to ensure the best and most long-lasting results, you must remain consistent in your efforts. You should eat healthily and take supplements every single day. When it comes to exercise, you should practice five days a week, giving your body two full days to rest and recover. You can choose to skip exercise when you go on vacation if the opportunity doesn't present itself; however, you must return to your regimen as soon as you get home.

Improving Your Shoulders and Arms

Once you get your overall physical appearance where it needs to be, you can start working on the more detailed aspects of creating an Alpha Male appearance. One of the main areas of focus needs to be on your shoulders and arms. After all, the broader your shoulders are, the more respect you will command just by walking into a room. This is one reason why men in uniform often appear larger than life. While the uniform itself adds a lot to their appearance, it is their broad shoulders filling out the uniform that actually attracts attention. Additionally, having strong, healthy arms will go a long way to making an impact wherever you are, especially when you wear a t-shirt or short sleeves showing off your advanced muscle tone.

Fortunately, several easy exercises will help you create Alpha Male shoulders and arms in no time. Again, your results will only be equal to your efforts; therefore, you must spend time every week working on your arms and shoulders by performing the right exercises. Overhead presses are an excellent exercise for building broad shoulders. It is important to perform them correctly, using your arms and shoulders to lift the barbell and not your legs. Your legs should be straight at all times, thereby putting the focus of effort on your shoulders. Five sets of five repetitions each are all you need to do to start building the shoulders of your dreams.

Upright rows are another good exercise for building broad, strong shoulders. This is similar to an overhead press, but instead of pushing the barbell up over your head from shoulder height, you pull it up to your chin from your waist. You can choose to use a single dumbbell in each hand for both exercises if you need time to build your strength. Additionally, using dumbbells is safer if you have to exercise alone; any time you use barbells, especially with heavy weights, it is recommended that you work out with at least one partner who can spot you and help you to avoid injury.

Lateral raises and farmer's carries are two other exercises recommended for building strong shoulders. In the case of lateral raises, you will raise dumbbells from your waist to shoulder height, keeping your arms straight. As the name suggests, these raises are done with your arms pointing out at your sides. The farmer's carry is when you carry dumbbells at waist height, keeping your arms straight as you walk naturally. This puts the focus of the effort on your shoulders.

Exercises for building muscle tone in your arms are fairly common and well-known. Any bench press will help to increase muscle tone in your arms, as will any barbell curl exercise. Four of the best exercises to get you started are the close grip bench press, the standard barbell curl, triceps dips, and the hammer curl. These exercises will not only get your biceps well-formed; they will ensure that all muscles in your arms, shoulders and upper chest also get well-formed. Again, since these exercises require the use of a barbell, always work out with someone who will be able to assist you if something goes wrong.

Improving Your Waist and Legs

The last area you want to focus on is your upper body; you don't want to develop it first, leaving your waist and legs to look flimsy and weak. Therefore, you must implement exercises for your waist and legs before working on upper body, thereby giving your appearance a natural symmetry that will add to your visual appeal.

When it comes to shaping your waist, the most important thing to focus on is your diet. This is because your waistline is the first place where fat usually gets deposited. Only when you eat right will you have any chance of creating a waist that is appealing to others, and that gives you the confidence of an Alpha Male.

Several exercises can help you to trim your waistline down and keep it looking mean and lean for years to come. Ab wheel rollouts are one such exercise. An ab wheel is a piece of exercise equipment available at any gym. To do a rollout, you need to be on your knees, keeping your back straight or only slightly arched while slowly extending your upper body forward using the wheel. Hanging leg raises are another excellent exercise for trimming your waistline. Simply hang from a bar, much like you would if you were about to do chin-ups, but instead of lifting with your arms, bring your knees up to your chest. Although this sounds simple, it will work out your chest muscles, arm muscles, and shoulders in a very serious way.

Finally, there is the exercise known as the windshield wiper leg raise. This is where you lay on your back and lift your legs straight into the air, keeping them together and your knees straight. Then you move your legs from side to side while keeping your upper body in place. The motion looks a bit like windshield wipers going back and forth, hence the name.

Everyone's body is unique in a great many ways. One such way is that you will have certain muscle groups that are naturally stronger and better defined than others. For example, you might already have broad shoulders, or thick, muscular legs. Or, you might have strong arms or a slim stomach. The important thing is to invest your time and energy wisely. Therefore, spend less time developing the areas of your body already in decent shape. Instead, focus most of your time and effort on building your weaker areas. This will help to give you a more symmetrical look. You can choose to spend one day on all the exercises that focus on your strong points while taking individual days for each of the other areas that need more work.

Chapter 12: Alpha Male Habit # 5: Mental Toughness

While physical appearance can be all-important for making that first impression, it takes more than muscles to keep people, especially women, impressed for long. This is why Alpha Males possess an abundance of what is commonly referred to as mental toughness. Just as a strong body can remove many physical obstacles and withstand physical attacks, so too, a strong mind can overcome mental and emotional obstacles and withstand all sorts of negative assaults, both from without as well as from within. Mental toughness is the condition of having the strongest mind available, the kind of mind that can rise above any situation and prevail against all the odds. To achieve this mental toughness, you have to develop the habit of standing strong in your beliefs and pursuits. This chapter will discuss some of the key ways to achieve this goal, as well as the numerous advantages mental toughness will provide in all areas of your life.

Redefining Failure

Failure is something that every person experiences numerous times throughout their life. Unfortunately, it is also one of the most misunderstood situations that people face. Most see failure as the end of the road, where dreams and ambitions come crashing down in a fiery mess. They see failure as a painful experience that should be avoided at all costs. The result is that most people never step out of their comfort zone. This means that they choose a life of mediocrity rather than one where they turn their dreams into reality.

In contrast, Alpha Males are not only unafraid of leaving their comfort zone, they usually spend most of their existence there. This is because rather than fearing failure, Alphas embrace it. This might seem hard to understand at first, especially given the role that success plays in the life of an Alpha Male. However, it's how an Alpha embraces failure that makes all the difference. In the mind of an Alpha Male, failure isn't a painful experience, nor does it spell the end of a dream. Instead, it is a learning experience, one in which the

Alpha Male can grow stronger, wiser, and ultimately better. They redefine failure, turning it into something positive rather than a negative.

To develop the Alpha Male trait of mental toughness, you must redefine failure. The first way to do this is to stop seeing failure as the end of the journey. Imagine you are driving somewhere you have never been before. If you take a wrong turn and begin to get lost, you don't simply give up and go home. Instead, you turn around, go back to where you made the wrong turn, and choose a different direction. This is precisely how failure can be seen. It is a wrong turn of sorts. Instead of giving up on a dream simply because the path you chose didn't work out, simply go back to square one and choose a different path. It isn't about which route you take to get to your destination; it's about arriving at the destination. Never, ever let failure cause you to quit. That is one of the most important habits to form when it comes to mental toughness.

Another way to redefine failure is to see it as a learning experience. Every time you fail to achieve a goal, rather than taking it personally, see it as a chance to learn and improve. Again, it took Thomas Edison one thousand attempts before he successfully created the electric light bulb. Each time, rather than getting frustrated or embarrassed, he became curious. He took the time to learn what each failure had to teach. It wasn't enough to know that a certain prototype didn't work; he wanted to know why. This is what ultimately led him to create the one that brought him success.

You can do the same thing in your life. Each time you fail, take a step back and replay the video in your mind. Why did you fail? What did you do wrong? Once you figure that out, you can try again, making sure you don't make the same mistakes. If you get shot down when asking a woman out on a date, ask yourself where it went wrong. It won't take long to figure out when you lost control of the situation or when she lost interest. Figure out the words or the actions that failed and remove them from your next attempt. The same can be applied to job interviews that went wrong, public speeches that don't achieve your intended goal, or any other situation where failure occurs. Rather than giving up or losing confidence, take the opportunity to grow with every failure you encounter. Eventually, you will almost be happy when you fail because you will see it as an opportunity for personal growth.

Establishing Discipline

Another element of mental toughness is discipline. Imagine a person who has an entire gym at their disposal, with all the equipment, and even a staff of personal trainers on hand twenty-four hours a day, seven days a week. All of those resources are for nothing if the individual doesn't put in the effort to exercise on a regular basis. The element needed to turn resources into results is discipline.

One form of discipline that forms mental toughness is staying focused on the task at hand. All too often, people get distracted by any number of things, like their cell phone, social media, or even their own imagination. They allow their minds to wander, causing their productivity to dip and the quality of their results to suffer. In contrast, an Alpha Male exercises great mental discipline, staying singularly focused on whatever task he is performing no matter how large or small, no matter how important or insignificant. That is one of the things that set the Alpha Male apart from everyone else. He will put one hundred percent of his attention and effort into every single thing he does. This ensures he has greater productivity and that he produces the best results every time. Eliminate all distractions whenever you address a task, and invest all of your effort into anything you do.

Another type of discipline that Alpha Males possess is that of emotional discipline. This is what an Alpha uses to avoid reacting to something in an emotionally charged way. It can be all too easy to snap at someone who says the wrong thing, especially when you are stressed out because things aren't going according to plan. What sets Alpha Males apart is that rather than letting their emotions get the best of them, they always keep their emotions in check. One way is to stop letting things affect you personally. Don't let what other people say or do change your mood; don't allow others to impact your emotional wellbeing. Let them say or do what they want. The trick is to stay focused on your opinions, your vision, and most importantly, your beliefs. Just because they don't agree with you doesn't mean you aren't right. Additionally, it's not your job to get them to see things your way. Live your life according to *your* vision and *your* rules, and let the rest of the world do *their* thing.

Finally, there is the aspect of discipline regarding how you manage your time. In a world filled with all sorts of distractions and responsibilities, it can be all too easy to get swept up in the momentum of life. When this happens, it causes a person to lose their sense of direction and perspective. Sometimes they aren't sure where they are going, and they never seem to have enough time to get there. Alpha Males will always seem to be in charge of their life, rather than a hapless victim of it. This is because they create a schedule that keeps them from getting swept away by the fast pace of modern-day life. When you create a daily routine, including when you go to bed, when you wake up, and when you perform your functions throughout the day, you create a sense of order that eliminates the stress and chaos that affect countless people every day. This discipline of time management enables you to spend quality time doing the things that matter most, such as spending time with loved ones and family, focusing on personal development, and chasing your dreams and ambitions. It's not about finding the right time to do things; it's about using your time in the right way to get everything done.

Staying Positive

The final habit to form when it comes to developing mental toughness is that of staying positive. Even the strongest, smartest, and most capable of Alpha Males will have bad days. Things don't always go according to plan, people can be negative and toxic, and situations can arise that test even the strongest of resolves. These things are unavoidable; however, this doesn't mean that those bad times have to change who you are. This is one of the most important lessons in the life of an Alpha Male: never let events define you, always be the author of who you are.

One way to always control your identity is to stay positive no matter what. A good way to do this is to remember that no matter how bad times get, they are temporary. It's a bit like the weather. Even the fiercest storm will end eventually, giving way to sunny, peaceful days once again. Alpha Males know this, and that is how they manage to stay calm and positive no matter how bad things get. They know that you can't control bad times any more than you can control the weather, so they don't lose energy trying to do so. They also know that it gets darkest before dawn, so even the worst of times will give way to better times once again.

Another reason Alpha Males stay positive is that they don't fear the worst times. Sure, bad times can have devastating effects on anyone's life. However, Alpha Males know that they can rebuild their lives no matter how much devastation they face. Furthermore, they take such opportunities to rebuild their lives better than they were before. It's a bit like if a house gets destroyed by a tornado. Rather than getting all emotional and bitter about it, an Alpha Male will see it as a chance to build an even better house. This is similar to redefining failure. When you see even the darkest, most tragic events as a chance for self-improvement, you will maintain a positive mindset as you look to the future and see how much better things will be as a result of those darker times. Therefore, rather than focusing on the negative aspect of an event, learn to focus on the positive results such events can lead to. This will keep your mood positive and buoyant no matter what situation you find yourself in, thus enabling you to see things clearly and remain in control of your actions while others flounder around you.

Chapter 13: Alpha Male Habit # 6: Charm

A common trait often associated with being an Alpha Male is that of arrogance. This association is completely mistaken, and it paints Alpha Male's in a negative light. Arrogantly bragging about your abilities and achievements (usually while belittling others in the process) demonstrates insecurity and jealousy, traits that are not consistent with the Alpha Male mindset. True Alpha Males demonstrate another trait when interacting with others, one that reveals their unrivaled strength of character. This is the trait of charm. Whether it is in appearance, approach, or how they speak, Alpha Males will exude charm in every way imaginable. Therefore, to further your Alpha Male development, you must master the art of charm. This habit will ensure others see you as a confident, capable Alpha Male standing head and shoulders above the rest.

Instilling Charm in Your Appearance

As already mentioned in this book, your appearance is almost always the first element of your personality others discover. Therefore, if you allow your appearance to be sloppy and unimpressive, you put yourself in a negative position when interacting with others. Since their first impression of you will be unfavorable, you will have to rely on your other qualities to dig yourself out of the hole you put yourself in. This is why it is vital to ensure that your appearance gets your interactions off to the right start, one where you are respected and admired even before you have opened your mouth.

Fortunately, it takes little effort to instill charm into your appearance. The first thing you want to do is get rid of any clothes that are dingy, worn, oversized, or just sloppy in appearance. Being casual doesn't mean you have to look homeless. Instead of opting for worn-out sneakers, invest in some comfortable, well-made shoes that combine aesthetics with comfort and function. You should always look at ease wherever you are, whatever you are doing; the right shoes will help you achieve that look while also telling others that you have an eye for style and fashion.

The same goes for all of your clothing. Don't settle for a floppy sweatshirt that advertises the store from which it was purchased. That won't set you apart from the crowd in any way. Instead, invest in shirts that stand out, whether it's the color, the cut, or the overall style. Always go for something as stylish as it is unique. Clothes don't have to just be about hiding your nakedness; they should be about expressing yourself. Treat them as the medium for your artistic flair. Choose shirts that flatter your shape and skin tone, and that show off your arms as you begin to develop your Alpha Male physique.

Pants should be seen in the same way. Rather than wearing baggy jeans that are as common as a ten-dollar haircut, opt for pants that provide a little more flair. You don't have to wear a suit and tie all the time, but a good pair of fashionable pants can make all the difference when it comes to being noticed for all the right reasons. You want your pants to accentuate your body's shape, so choose the colors and styles needed to make you look like the proverbial million dollars. This will mean you need to take the time to try on different options to ensure you get the most for your money. Don't expect the pair of pants on the skinny dude in the poster to work, necessarily. Instead, always recognize your body's shape and work with it accordingly. No matter what size or shape you are now, some clothes can give you the Alpha Male appearance that will turn heads wherever you go.

Instilling Charm in Your Approach

In addition to affecting how you look, charm can make all the difference when it comes to your approach. This is true in every area, including approaching a woman, a potential boss, a potential client, or any other person. Being an Alpha Male affects every aspect of your life. It's not as though you turn it on when it matters and turn it off when it doesn't. One of the secrets that make Alpha Males so successful is that they are the same twenty-four hours a day, seven days a week. So, your approach needs to be one of charm and poise no matter whether you are trying to attract a woman or pay the guy who mows your lawn.

Before forming any new habits in this area, the first thing you need to do is ensure you don't have any bad habits. Being too needy is one such bad habit that needs to be eliminated right away. Never appear desperate when it comes to achieving your goal, no matter how important that goal is. Neediness and desperation are signs of weakness. Instead, exercise patience. Always approach a person or situation with calm confidence, the sort of attitude that tells them that while you are confident of success, you won't be intimidated if things don't turn out the way you expect.

How you walk is one way to demonstrate this attitude. Never appear as though you are rushing around like a madman, running from one obligation to another. Instead, develop a walk that is both purposeful and relaxed. Long, natural strides will give you an air of authority, while a slow but steady pace will give you an air of relaxed confidence. Neither hurried nor sluggish, this walk will set you apart from the rest who are usually running around like the proverbial chickens with their heads cut off.

How you carry yourself is equally important when it comes to mastering the art of charm. No one takes the "macho man" image seriously, so walking around like a gym junky on steroids won't get the attention you desire. Instead, you should maintain an upright posture while keeping your body fairly relaxed. Your arms should hang loosely down by your side when standing and should swing freely but not excessively when walking. A good rule of thumb is always to feel balanced. When you are walking, you should feel as though you could stop suddenly without falling either forward or backward. Alternatively, when you are standing, you should feel relaxed yet firm, as though someone could push you unexpectedly and not knock you over. Keeping your feet apart is a good way to achieve this balance. Also, always keep your shoulders square and your chin up as this will give you an added air of command.

Instilling Charm in How You Speak

The final area where you need to master the art of charm is in how you speak. Just as the pace with which you walk says everything about you, so too, the pace with which you speak will tell others who you really are. How you say your words can prove just as important as the words themselves. When you speak too quickly, it demonstrates anxiety; speaking too slow can suggest that you are disinterested, or worse, a bit stupid. To demonstrate confidence, intelligence, and ultimately charm, you need to learn to speak in a calm yet purposeful pace, one in which your words are enunciated and deliberate. Your speech should feel as balanced as your stride.

What you say can make or break you in the eyes, or ears, of others. Many men fall into the trap of trying to use fancy words to impress others. They either wind up using words incorrectly or even worse, they use big, fancy words correctly but only confuse those they are speaking to. Therefore, focus on the content rather than the words themselves. Only use words you fully understand and are comfortable with. The important thing is to express yourself clearly and thoroughly. Anything else is just wasted and makes it appear as though you are trying to impress someone.

Another element of charm within speech is that of offering compliments. Whether you are telling a woman that she is beautiful or telling the lawn guy that he did a tremendous job, paying someone a sincere, heartfelt compliment will always come across as charming. However, the key is that a compliment has to be sincere. Rather than just saying something shallow and mundane such as "You look beautiful today," you will want to focus on a particular quality, such as "That color really brings out the color of your eyes," or "Those shoes really look adorable on you." When you take the time to add details to your compliment, they tell the other person that you are sincere in your words, and that makes all the difference between a compliment and a pick-up line or shallow attempt at ingratiation.

Perhaps the most important aspect of charm when it comes to speaking is that of knowing when not to speak. Anyone who tries to dominate the conversation will be seen as overbearing or bullying, qualities that don't attract positive reactions. In contrast, when a man sits silently, his eyes fixed on the person speaking, it gives an air of respect, interest, and true connection. Sometimes the best way into a woman's heart isn't the words you say, or even how you say them, but it is the ability to stay silent while listening intently to what *she* has to say. Good eye contact, relaxed nods, and a genuine smile or frown at the appropriate time will convey that you are sincerely listening to her, not zoning out wondering who will win tonight's game or whether she has a prettier sister. This is how you can remain active in a conversation without having to say a single word.

Chapter 14: Alpha Male Habit # 7: Purpose

Another vital habit practiced by all Alpha Males is that of living by core values and staying true to purpose. All of the charm, confidence, and skill in the world won't amount to much if you don't have good reason to put them to use. This is where purpose comes into play. In essence, purpose is the direction you travel in when living your life. Without purpose, you simply drift along, letting the current take you where it will. However, when you have a purpose, it's like having a compass that you can use to ensure your actions and circumstances are taking you where you want to go. Purpose can also embody your core values. By taking the time to discover and develop your personal values, you ensure that your actions and efforts will always be consistent, providing stability and reliability in your life. Not only will that help you to achieve your goals, but it will also make you stand out in the eyes of others. The more reliable and constant you are, the more others will trust and respect you.

Discovering Your Core Values

The first step toward developing purpose in your life is to take the time to discover your core values. Most people are so fixated on achieving success or impressing others that they will do anything necessary to realize those goals. This leaves them feeling empty and uncertain when it comes to their own beliefs and desires. In contrast, an Alpha Male has a clear set of core values that tells him who he is, what he wants, and what he is willing to do to accomplish his goals. Such a values system not only sets the Alpha Male up for success, but it also gives him strength, hope, and courage in times of failure and distress.

Discovering your core values requires a fair bit of soul searching. Therefore, take as much time and effort as is needed to conscientiously accomplish this task. An important element of this task is to write everything down. Rather than grabbing the nearest scrap of paper or partially used napkin, give this the respect it deserves and buy a proper journal. Devote this journal to your personal development as an Alpha Male and as a person in general. Although some may see keeping a journal as effeminate or nerdy, the truth of the matter is that the strongest, most successful people keep journals almost religiously.

Once you have your journal and pen, set aside some time to sit and contemplate. Make sure you will be undisturbed and turn off all distractions, including your phone, the TV, and even the radio. Next, write down the question, "What am I passionate about?" If those words don't kick your mind into action, you can create a different question, such as "What makes me truly happy?" or "What do I want most in life?" or "If I had ten million dollars what would I do?" In short, you are trying to find the things that give you meaning, true happiness, and that make your life worthwhile. When you have the question that works for you, take the time to listen to what pops into your mind. Write everything down, no matter how ridiculous it may seem. This isn't a test, nor is it something that anyone else ever has to see. Therefore, be honest and don't hold back. Write down everything that comes into your mind.

Next, reduce your list to about five items. Chances are that any more than five are the result of external influences, a passing interest, or redundant interests. All in all, you should only have up to five or six things that truly inspire you, things you would pursue if money were no object. If you have trouble with reducing your list, then try to prioritize it in order of importance. If you still can't get your list down to five simply break the list in half, taking the top five for values to focus on now and the others as values to address later on down the road.

The values you list shouldn't be goals as such; rather, they should be the values that underlie your goals. Therefore, marrying a particular person or finding a specific job aren't values. Having a happy home life or a satisfying career, however, are. The following is a short list of values that will help get you started:

- ✔ Discipline
- ✔ Freedom
- ✔ Happiness

- ✔ Spirituality
- ✔ Fun
- ✔ Physical health and wellbeing
- ✔ Knowledge
- ✔ Power
- ✔ Financial stability
- ✔ Success
- ✔ Family
- ✔ Self-expression
- ✔ Integrity

Defining Yourself by Your Values

Once you have listed your values, the next step is to separate your list into two categories. One category will be those values such as integrity, discipline, knowledge, and the like that define you as a person. The other category will be such values as financial stability, physical health and wellbeing, freedom and the like that define the life you want to live. When you have divided your list, you are ready to begin defining yourself based on your values.

Next, write down your personal values on a fresh page. Now, try to imagine a role model that personifies those qualities. There might be someone in your personal life that possesses them in abundance, or you might choose a character in literature, the movies or religious texts. Again, since this isn't a test, there is no wrong answer. Instead, this is about you finding your ideal. It doesn't matter who personifies that idea. All that matters is that you have that ideal clear in your mind so that you can measure your words and actions accordingly. If your ideal is Superman, then you have Superman in your mind. Any time you find yourself in a challenging situation you simply ask yourself, "What would Superman do?" This will bring your values to mind, ensuring that your actions are consistent with integrity, discipline, and knowledge.

It's not about becoming Superman, rather it's about becoming your ideal self. Eventually, you won't need an icon to embody your values. Instead, you will embody them so thoroughly that you only need to ask yourself what *you* would do, and those values will be right there. Alternatively, you might not even have to ask the question at all. Your values will be so ingrained in your character that you will only have to act naturally to do the right thing. The best part is that as you become your ideal self, others will look to you for inspiration, using your example to become their best self.

Still, this isn't about impressing others or becoming the hero. Instead, this is about establishing your values for your own peace of mind. So much stress and anxiety revolve around guilt and uncertainty, things that come when values are either ignored or simply unknown. When you take the time to discover and implement your values, you create a life that is honest and true, one that provides peace of mind and a clear conscience. This is at the very heart of being an Alpha Male. When you live by your values, you have the strength of character that keeps you safe, and that makes you stand out from those who flounder around aimlessly as they struggle to find their way.

Establishing Your Purpose

The other half of your list will be those values that best define your life, such as financial stability, physical health and wellbeing, and freedom. Although these values affect who you are as a person, they tend to describe your lifestyle rather than your core beliefs. Physical health and wellbeing require you to exercise and eat right, things that are part of your lifestyle, unlike integrity, which stems from a state of mind. These are the values that establish your purpose. Write these values in your journal on a separate page and envision the lifestyle that personifies them. You can use the lifestyle of someone you know, a famous person, or something that is of your own creation. All that matters is that you create an image of the reality you wish to achieve. This will give you a destination to pursue, and this destination will become your purpose.

When your life has a purpose, it has direction. This helps you to make better and easier decisions throughout life. For example, deciding what job to pursue becomes far easier when you have a sense of direction. If a job takes you closer to financial stability and freedom, then it is a good fit for you. Alternatively, if it fails to provide those elements, then it is a bad fit as it takes you further away from the life you want to create.

This sense of purpose helps you to be in constant control of your life. By knowing what your dreams are, and thus what it will take to make those dreams come true, you know immediately whether something is good or bad just by its very nature. Furthermore, your personal values will help you to stay true to your principles as you plot a course that takes you to your ultimate destination, the life of your dreams. Every choice and decision you make will be purpose-driven, and this will give you the confidence and certainty that most people lack, making you the true Alpha Male in the group.

Chapter 15: Alpha Male Habit # 8: Self-Care

Numerous studies have shown a direct and significant link between self-care and self-esteem. When a person puts time and effort into their appearance and overall wellbeing every day, their self-esteem is strong and healthy. When people ignore their appearance and spend little to no time taking care of their personal needs, their self-esteem plummets. In fact, one sure way to help a person overcome depression is to force them to spend time grooming daily. Sadly, a study done in 2017 by AXE revealed that most men between the ages of 18 to 30 feel pressured by the "macho" image to ignore grooming and other forms of self-care since such things are considered effeminate. Common stereotypes suggest that tough men don't care about their image, causing many to equate grubbiness with masculinity. Alpha Males, by contrast, recognize the importance of self-care in all its forms. Therefore, a necessary habit to form when developing the Alpha Male lifestyle is to take care of yourself, both internally and externally. This chapter will reveal ways to achieve this goal, helping you to create a daily regimen that will cultivate your Alpha Male mindset.

Physical Self-Care

The first element of self-care that you need to establish is that of physical self-care. This covers a wide array of responsibilities, but they are all equally vital in terms of creating an Alpha Male lifestyle. As already discussed, the first step is to watch what you eat, with regard to both what types of food and how much food. Also, note that eating late at night has been proven to increase body fat and even adversely affect your sleep patterns, leaving you sluggish and tired the next day. Always make sure that you eat a healthy meal at least three hours before you plan on going to bed; this will ensure your body digests your food before shutting down to get the rest it needs.

Another element of physical self-care that is often overlooked is bathing. It is vital to shower each and every day, not just to avoid unpleasant odors but also to keep your body healthy and germ-free. The longer you go between showers, the less likely your body will be able to fight common sicknesses such as the cold or flu. Additionally, your skin can begin to suffer numerous consequences when you skip bathing, such as an increase in acne, clogged pores, and even rapid aging due to dehydration. This leads to another important issue, namely using hydrating soaps and lotions when you bathe. Avoid anything that claims to be shampoo and body wash all in one. Such items will only dry your scalp and skin, leaving you worse off after a shower than before. Use soaps and shampoos that restore moisture to skin and hair, as these will improve your physical appearance significantly.

Finally, there is the practice of pampering your body. Get massages regularly. Go to saunas or hot tubs to relax your muscles and soothe your mind. Although these practices seem indulgent, they are, in fact, essential for a healthy body and mind. Massages can do wonders when it comes to maintaining healthy muscles, blood flow, and oxygen flow throughout your body. Additionally, they help you to unwind in a way that makes stress and anxiety virtually evaporate from your body and mind. Since Alpha Males aren't worried about public perception when it comes to masculinity, they will get massages and even take bubble baths to ensure a happier and healthier state of physical wellbeing.

Mental Self-Care

Just as the body requires exercise to become healthy and strong, the mind requires its own type of exercise to thrive. Unfortunately, this is another area that many men ignore due to misguided stereotypes that imply "manly men" are never supposed to be seen with a book in their hands or wandering the galleries of a museum. Such "manly men", although physically strong, will remain mentally weak. Alpha Males know that to truly impress a woman, you need to have brains as well as brawn; therefore, they spend as much time and effort exercising their mind as they do their body.

Reading is one of the best mental exercises you can do. Reading ten to fifteen minutes per day is all it takes to boost your mental health, and is something that you can do any time of day and in any place, provided there is enough light and you can tune out the surrounding noise and distractions. Perhaps the best part of reading is that it provides countless conversations regarding the genres you like, the topics you read, and how those things affect your life. This will keep you interesting far after the "manly men" have lost their luster in a woman's eyes.

Learning new things can also go a long way to creating and maintaining mental health and wellbeing. Not only has learning been proven to improve memory and problem-solving skills, but it has also been shown to stave off such things as Alzheimer's and other disorders that affect people late in life. One of the most effective tools in this area is learning another language. Few things are as attractive as a man who can speak more than one language, so this is a win/win situation, to say the least. In addition to improving your mental acuity by learning another language, you will also really impress your lady by ordering dinner in the native language of the restaurant you take her to on date night. Not only will your woman admire you for your intellect, but the women around will also take note (usually to the detriment of their significant other).

Learning a new language requires only ten to fifteen minutes a day and can be done online at no cost. Trips to museums or other intellectually charged environments can be made once every couple of weeks or so, giving you a more intensive dose of mental exercise that helps develop the mind of a true Alpha Male.

Emotional Self-Care

Emotional self-care is something that can make all the difference when it comes to your overall state of mind. The more stressed and frustrated you are, the less confident and self-assured you will be. Therefore, you must spend time every day taking care of your emotional needs, much the way you do when it comes to taking care of your physical needs.

Effective emotional care is a two-sided coin. On the one side, the most important thing you can do to improve your emotional health and wellbeing is to control the information that goes into your mind. In other words, avoid input that causes you anxiety or distress as much as possible. An excellent example of this is watching the news. Unfortunately, most men associate watching the news with keeping in touch with the world around them. The truth of the matter is that most news channels focus on sensational stories, often embellishing them to increase the "wow factor." This means that rather than staying on top of current affairs, you are simply subjecting yourself to stressful, frustrating stories that are designed to elicit an emotional response. The solution is to avoid watching the news every single day, choosing instead to limit your exposure to once or twice a week. Furthermore, be selective on the sources you use to get your information. Choose sources that stick to the facts rather than opinions that are aimed at getting you emotionally charged.

The other side of the coin is that of seeking out things that provide positive emotional responses. In other words, do things that make you happy. If watching sporting events makes you happy, then do that. In fact, rather than settling for watching your favorite team on TV, take the time and effort to buy season tickets to watch them play in the flesh. This will take the experience to a whole new level, one that provides you and your loved ones the best results possible. If sporting events aren't your thing, but going to the movies, hobbies, gardening, fishing, or any other similar activity is what works then do that thing and do it well. Get the best gear, treat yourself to all the perks, spare no expense. After all, the more you invest in your happiness, the happier you will be.

Spiritual Self-Care

Finally, there is the aspect of spiritual self-care. This is another area where modern-day stereotypes serve to undermine a person's chances of true success. "Manly men" are supposed to be the self-reliant, grab-life-by-the-horns, conquer-the-world type of people who have little time for self-reflection and no need for contemplation. However, any true Alpha Male will attest to the fact that your values and beliefs are where you will find strength when you need it the most. This means that you need to take the time to develop and nurture your values and beliefs daily.

One way to achieve this goal is to find a practice that enables you to reflect on things. The things you reflect on can change from one day to the next, depending on circumstances. You might reflect on a particularly challenging situation at work for as long as it takes to resolve the issue. You might want to reflect on how to go about pursuing the girl or job of your dreams. There may be times when you do personal introspection, allowing you to contemplate who you are and where you are going. This will ensure that you always have a firm grasp on your life and that you avoid drifting aimlessly through life like countless people do every day.

Meditation is an easy and effective practice that can allow you to reflect or to clear your mind altogether if that is your choice. Numerous forms of meditation allow you to find the one that works best for you. Some are designed to release stress and anxiety, while others are more focused on clearing your mind and detaching from the outside world. Like physical exercise, you don't have to choose only one. Instead, you can mix it up and practice the form of meditation that best suits your needs at any particular moment. It only takes ten to fifteen minutes a day to meditate, meaning you can incorporate the practice into your daily routine without any problems at all.

Chapter 16: Setting Alpha Male Goals

So far, this book has provided all of the tools, insights, and directions you need to begin transforming your life into that of a true Alpha Male. However, there is one more piece of the puzzle that needs to be put in place before the big picture can be realized. That piece is setting goals. The importance of setting goals simply cannot be overstated. While many believe that the reasons they are unable to turn their dreams into reality are a lack of resources, time, or energy, the simple truth is that most people fall short due to a lack of goals. Goals are what turn dreams into achievable tasks, actions that can be taken daily to reach the desired destination. In short, goals are what turn abstract, intangible dreams into quantifiable reality. Therefore, to change your life in any way, shape or form, you must begin by setting the necessary goals. This chapter will discuss the nature of goals, as well as effective ways to set reasonable and achievable goals, thereby giving you the final element needed for creating the lifestyle of an Alpha Male.

What Exactly Is A Goal?

Many people mistakenly associate dreams with goals. Therefore, if you want to be rich, you might say your goal is to be rich. Unfortunately, this isn't entirely accurate. It would be more correct to say that your dream is to be rich. The goal is the step or set of steps in the plan that will lead you to that outcome. Knowing the destination is just the first step; it is the step of knowing your dream.

The next step is deciding how you will get there. You probably need to plot your journey. You may have to stop once or twice, depending on how far you have to go. How long it will take, which paths to choose, and whether you need to stop along the way are all part of planning the journey. This is the act of setting goals. Each path you enter is a goal, and each stop is a goal; every element of the journey, including when you leave, and when you return, are all goals. They are measurable actions that will lead you to your dream.

This is where most people fall short. By mistaking the dream for a goal, they never take the time to plot the course that will take them to where they want to be. They usually never even take the first step, since they are unsure as to which step to take. When you have your course plotted, you know where to go and when to go, allowing you to effectively take the actions needed to achieve your dream.

Methods for Effective Goal Setting

As with anything else in life, simply setting goals isn't always enough. Instead, you need to set the right goals in the right way. This will make all the difference when it comes to actually achieving the goals you set. Fortunately, there is a simple formula for effective goal setting, known as the SMARTER goal system, and it works like this:

- **S**pecific: Make sure always to set specific goals. Instead of saying you want to lose weight, set the goal of reaching a target weight, such as one hundred and eighty pounds. This is a specific goal in which you can easily track your progress.

- **M**easurable: The next step is to set a measurable goal. In the case of reaching a target weight, you need to measure where that weight is from where you currently are. Thus, if you weigh two hundred pounds, then your measurable goal is to lose twenty pounds.

- **A**ctionable: This is where you begin to plot your course with regard to achieving your overall goal. If you want to lose twenty pounds, you can set actions such as eating healthier foods or exercising more regularly. This turns the goal from an ambition into an achievable action.

- **R**ealistic: Sometimes, people make the mistake of setting goals that are too large to achieve. In the case of losing twenty pounds, you might choose to break the goal down into four smaller goals of losing five pounds per week. This takes the stress out of an "all or nothing" scenario, giving you easier targets to reach.

- **T**ime-bound: This part of goal setting has two elements. The first element is when you start. If you want to lose weight, decide on when you will start taking action. The next element is the deadline. This is when you hope to achieve your goal. Thus, your goal should now be to lose five pounds in one week, starting tomorrow.

- **Evaluate:** When you have your measurable goal and your timeframe, you can begin evaluating your progress. If you have only lost one pound halfway through your seven-day deadline, then you can look at either increasing your efforts, perhaps by engaging in more exercise or eating better, or extending the deadline. In the end, it's always better to alter the goal than to give up on it altogether.

- **Reward:** The final phase of goal setting is to reward yourself for the progress you make. For example, each time you lose five pounds, you can choose to reward yourself by purchasing that DVD you have wanted for awhile, or some other relatively inexpensive item that acts as an incentive. Not only will this encourage you to keep going, but it will also program your mind to crave achieving the goals you set. When you achieve the big goal, you can go clothes shopping as a reward, treating yourself to a new wardrobe that will show off your new look.

Setting SMARTER goals increases your chances of achieving those goals, and that will change your life in a couple of very significant ways. First, your self-confidence will grow stronger and stronger with every goal you achieve. Therefore, as you achieve more goals, you will grow in confidence, giving you the courage to chase more and larger goals. The second way that this will change your life is that it will increase your success overall. Each goal will improve your life in some way. Therefore, as you accomplish more goals, you will be eager to set even more goals, which will improve your life exponentially, enabling you to create the life of your dreams.

Specific Goals for The Alpha Male

Now that you know the importance of goals and how to go about setting them, the final step is to set goals that are specific for an Alpha Male. The following are some goals that will help you to develop the Alpha Male lifestyle you both desire and deserve:

- **Improve your Image:** As we discussed, this takes many forms, including the clothes you wear, your physique, and even your grooming habits. Therefore, you must break this overall goal down into smaller, more manageable goals. The first will be to improve your hairstyle. Give yourself thirty days to find a stylist who will help you to achieve the look that is right for you. Next, you will want to work on getting your weight to an ideal level. Give yourself thirty days to achieve a specific weight (if that is a goal that is achievable in this timeframe). Finally, you will want to improve your wardrobe. Give yourself another thirty days to change your clothing style, giving you the Alpha Male look that will attract all the right attention. Make this your last step, as you will want to be at your right weight and have a hairstyle ready to define which clothes work best for you.

- **Improve your Self-Image:** This is another goal that will have many aspects. One aspect is that of establishing your values. Take a week or two to carefully contemplate those things that truly define who you are and the life you want to live. Once you have chosen your values, you need to integrate them into your day to day life in the form of the choices you make and the actions you perform. Next, increase your positivity. Begin spending time around positive people, feeding off of their energy, and using them as inspiration for chasing your dreams. Finally, take thirty days to work on developing your charm. The more charming you act, the more charming you will feel. This will increase your self-esteem as well as your self-confidence when interacting with other people.

- **Chase your Dreams:** Once you have improved yourself inside and out, it is time to start turning your dreams into reality. Take some time to decide what you want to achieve. If it is winning the perfect woman, landing the perfect job, or achieving some other life-changing ambition, make that your purpose. Once you have chosen your purpose, start setting goals on how to reach that destination. Give yourself thirty days to come up with a destination and a solid plan on how to reach that destination. Use the SMARTER method to break your overall goal into smaller, more achievable goals that can be measured and tracked effectively. Now that you have developed the heart, mind, and appearance of a true Alpha Male, there is no dream beyond your reach. Now you can start creating the life you have always wanted, the life of your dreams.

Conclusion

Now that you have read this book, you have all the insights and tools you need to begin your journey toward becoming an Alpha Male. From identifying and overcoming those elements that have robbed you of self-esteem to developing the habits needed to increase your overall sense of self-worth, you can now transform your self-esteem into the vibrant and robust one only found in an Alpha Male. Furthermore, by following the proven techniques provided, you can form the habits that will increase your self-confidence, thereby giving you the drive and ambition needed to pursue and achieve your goals. Finally, you now have the methods and techniques needed to establish clear and achievable goals, the sort that will enable you to turn your dreams into reality by giving you the ability to pursue those dreams in a realistic and meaningful way. Whether you dream of landing the perfect job, of attracting the perfect wife, or of living a life that makes you stand out from the rest, you now have everything you need to make those dreams come true. The very best of luck on your journey to becoming an Alpha Male and creating the successful life you both desire and deserve!

Check out another book by Kory Heaton

Sources

https://themighty.com/2018/10/low-self-esteem-habits/

https://www.telegraph.co.uk/health-fitness/living-with-erectile-dysfunction/why-men-lack-confidence/

https://guycounseling.com/men-destroy-self-esteem/

https://conqueryourconfidence.com/10-signs-of-low-self-esteem-in-men-how-to-overcome-insecurities/

https://brightside.me/wonder-people/10-secret-fears-90-of-men-never-talk-about-386910/

https://goodmenproject.com/guy-talk/signs-of-an-insecure-man-cmtt/

https://goodmenproject.com/featured-content/19-men-reveal-what-their-biggest-insecurities-are-when-it-comes-to-dating/

https://www.youtube.com/watch?v=ZCvle-Loc50

https://www.devex.com/news/how-self-doubt-manifests-in-men-versus-women-92506,

https://www.realmenrealstyle.com/overcome-self-doubt/

https://conqueryourconfidence.com/10-signs-of-low-self-esteem-in-men-how-to-overcome-insecurities/

https://www.youtube.com/watch?v=beg57qXMZTE

https://www.psychologytoday.com/us/blog/mind-your-body/201810/positive-body-image-in-men,

https://www.mirror-mirror.org/body-image-men.htm

https://www.huffingtonpost.co.uk/jessica-lovejoy/body-image-issues-in-men_b_5514957.html?

https://www.intechopen.com/books/weight-loss/men-s-body-image-the-effects-of-an-unhealthy-body-image-on-psychological-behavioral-and-cognitive-he

https://goodmenproject.com/featured-content/5-life-changing-habits-that-build-self-esteem-cmtt/
https://www.irreverentgent.com/self-confidence-for-men/
https://www.youtube.com/watch?v=s2aFCuzeab4
https://www.youtube.com/watch?v=SAXwtyl0MEs
https://www.youtube.com/watch?v=yMCHgxLyoRQ
https://www.youtube.com/watch?v=2c4Jz41IZmk,
https://understandingrelationships.com/women-prefer-alpha-males/35905,
https://www.youtube.com/watch?v=kFSAe7X8Nls
https://www.knowledgeformen.com/how-to-be-an-alpha-male/
https://www.youtube.com/watch?v=vFg20vvN5H4
https://www.youtube.com/watch?v=PzB92OQzKG4
http://chadhowsefitness.com/2012/10/stop-being-a-pussy-persist/
https://heartiste.org/2012/12/17/persistence-the-underrated-alpha-male-quality/
https://www.youtube.com/watch?v=QGvmAhcNRuU
https://www.youtube.com/watch?v=O7xuL7gAM5w
https://therationalmale.com/2011/10/12/frame/
http://oldschool-calisthenic.ro/alpha-male-look/
https://brobible.com/sports/article/building-alpha-male-physique/
https://www.youtube.com/watch?v=4fcxxeefmTk
https://www.youtube.com/watch?v=dqXZYDGORos
https://themaaximumlife.com/mental-toughness-is-the-key-to-becoming-a-manly-man/
https://theartofcharm.com/confidence/become-alpha-male-staying-gentleman/
https://get-a-wingman.com/alpha-male-body-language-hacks-that-instantly-boost-your-attractiveness/
https://www.youtube.com/watch?v=TPSsLb8HNoE

https://www.guysplaybook.com/alpha-males-have-clear-purpose/
https://www.artofmanliness.com/articles/30-days-to-a-better-man-day-1-define-your-core-values/

https://www.vibe.com/2019/06/masculinity-and-self-care-feature
https://goodmenproject.com/featured-content/7-better-self-care-tips-for-guys-wcz/

https://www.youtube.com/watch?v=kSVqu9uK1hw,

https://www.youtube.com/watch?v=XpKvs-apvOs,

https://productcoalition.com/how-to-hack-goal-setting-for-more-confidence-31ecdaa4deea, https://www.knowledgeformen.com/goal-setting/

https://www.thebabereport.com/6-reasons-why-women-love-dating-direct-men/

https://www.irreverentgent.com/how-to-look-more-handsome-and-attractive/

https://www.glidedesign.com/12-examples-of-persistence-paying-off/

www.ingramcontent.com/pod-product-compliance
Lightning Source LLC
Chambersburg PA
CBHW070049230426
43661CB00005B/828